MINI-LATHE

FOR HOME MACHINISTS

DAVID FENNER

FOX CHAPEL
PUBLISHING

© 2012 by David Fenner and Fox Chapel Publishing Company, Inc., East Petersburg, PA.

First published in the United Kingdom by Special Interest Model Books, 2008.
First published in North America in 2012 by Fox Chapel Publishing, 1970 Broad Street,
East Petersburg, PA 17520.

ISBN 978-1-56523-695-0

Library of Congress Cataloging-in-Publication Data

Fenner, David, 1944-

Mini-lathe for home machinists / David Fenner.

    p. cm.

Includes index.

ISBN 978-1-56523-695-0

1. Turning (Lathe work) 2. Lathes. I. Title.

TT207.F46 2012

684'.083--dc23

                        2011042813

To learn more about the other great books from Fox Chapel Publishing, or to find a retailer near you,
call toll-free 800-457-9112 or visit us at *www.FoxChapelPublishing.com*.

Note to Authors: We are always looking for talented authors to write new books.
Please send a brief letter describing your idea to Acquisition Editor,
1970 Broad Street, East Petersburg, PA 17520.

Printed in China
Second printing

CONTENTS

Chapter 1

Safety

Before getting into the fun of working with a Mini-Lathe, a few words on the subject of workshop safety may be in order. In an industrial environment, many activities involving machine tools are governed by legislation aimed at improving health and safety. One of the delightful aspects of the personal hobby workshop lies in "escaping" from the worldly cares outside and as such, in our leisure pursuits, much of such legislation does not apply, and responsibility for safety of both ourselves and our visitors, lies very much in our own hands. A sensible approach to safe working practices involves first an appreciation of factors which can give rise to injury (and those parts of the body at risk), and second, a common sense attitude to working around these factors.

Fingers and hands

While a small machine such as the Mini-Lathe has much less power than a heavy-duty production machine, the motor is nevertheless rated at about a half horsepower. The inertia of chuck and work spinning at maximum speed would certainly be sufficient to cause severe damage to a misplaced finger. Another of the regular injuries is laceration due to sharp edges, which may be the tool, the work, or the swarf. Ribbons of swarf may look like bits of Xmas decoration, but think of then as long thin ragged razor blades. So when clearing swarf do not use fingers.

Eyes

Some materials, notably brass, produce swarf, which comes away in small needles at high velocity. If you have the misfortune to get some of this in an eye, then it is almost certainly a trip to hospital, where (being non-magnetic) it will be removed manually. Safety glasses are cheap and will prevent this. They should also be worn when grinding tools on the bench grinder.

Feet

In an engineering factory you might wear safety boot or shoes rated so that you could drive a car over your foot without damage to toes. In our amateur shop, most of what we handle will weigh perhaps a pound or two at most. A pound or half kilo dropped from bench height would cause a fair amount of bruising, so trainers or open toe style sandals may not be the ideal footwear. My version of Murphy's Law also states that if you drop a sharp edged object on to your foot, it will land sharp side down.

Hair

Long hair can be caught by a rotating shaft and wound in, leading to probable head or facial injury. Tie hair back or use a net.

General clothing

A tie presents the same form of risk as long hair. Preferably remove it or at least ensure that it is tucked in under a sweater. Loose fitting sleeves are similarly not recommended. Open collars can present a problem when machining at high speed. Hot swarf dropping down inside the neck can be painful and can cause involuntary movement leading to a secondary risk.

Electrical Safety

If you have purchased a new machine, then all should be well. If second hand, then it may be worth checking that the plug, cable and connections are in good order. If you are using an extension cable, route it in such a way that you won't trip over it. Connecting via an earth leakage or residual current circuit breaker is a sensible precaution.

Industrial machining processes often make extensive use of water based coolant to speed up the cutting. Clearly, water and electricity (especially at mains voltage) are not happy bedfellows. Using of the proprietary cutting compounds will be a safer option.

Chapter 2

Preparing the Lathe

Background and description

The version of the Mini-Lathe discussed in this book, is the one offered by Arc Euro Trade, who kindly made the machine available for assessment. Other suppliers in the UK such as Chester, Chronos, Machine Mart, Warco etc. offer similar machines, and although there may be detail differences, they are substantially the same machines. The detail differences usually relate to variations in motor power, length of bed, tailstock clamping mode, spindle tachometer, and DRO handwheels. Manufactured in China, it has been available for a number of years, and with the passage of time, the specification and range of accessories has improved in response to customer feedback. Arc offer machines either "Factory assembled" or "ARC prepared". The latter costs a little more but for the extra money, they strip, clean, and adjust the machine, so that on receipt it is ready for immediate use. The machine in this case is "Factory Assembled", so the preparation exercise, generally based on what is done by Arc will form the essence of this first chapter. They are now planning a picture storybook, which will be published, on their website in due course.

The catalogue description quotes: swing over bed 180mm and distance between centres 350mm or 13.78in. The swing figure is diameter rather than radius so the centre height would be 90mm or 3.54in. The spindle is bored through 20mm diameter, and carries a No.3 Morse Taper (MT3 Taper), the tailstock being MT2. The 80mm 3-jaw chuck is retained by three bolts, and bored through 16mm, while the optional 100mm 4-jaw chuck has a 22mm bore.

Power comes from a 350 watt (Approx. 1/2hp) D.C. motor with continuously variable speed. A two-speed gear system gives a claimed total range of 100 to 3000 rpm.

Over the years, the Myford ML7 has become almost the standard model engineer's lathe, so some comparisons are inevitable. The swing over bed is a few thou larger, but there is no bed gap; the length between centres is shorter (standard Myford is 19in.); spindle bore and taper are greater (15.08mm and MT3); weight is less at 44Kg compared to the older S7 at 111Kg. Notably, the cross slide is relatively short; this with the associated make up, places a restriction on the radial movement available at the toolpost. As for price, a brand new Mini lathe will set you back around £500 and for the same money you might be lucky to get a well-worn ML7. Looking at the small footprint and fairly low weight, this might well be a machine that could be tucked away in a corner of a spare bedroom rather than a draughty workshop. My guess is that it will appeal to newcomers to the hobby making a first purchase, and to those working in small scale or on small components.

It was noted above that the machine, in various guises, has been around for some years, and has sold in large numbers, notably in the US market. Many owners have been modifying and improving machines, and much information is available on the Internet. In particular the Frank Hoose site www.mini-lathe.com is most informative and carries a wide variety of links.

Delivery

The machine was delivered by overnight carrier in two packages strapped together. These were separated after moving into the workshop. Here the elevating barrow came into its own, making light of moving from delivery van along the gravel driveway to workshop. The lathe comes housed in and bolted to the base of, a plywood packing case. My chosen sequence was to remove the top and one side, **(Photo 2.1)** then remove the bolts. The barrow platform was then raised so that it became an easy matter to slide the machine across on to the bench; **(Photo 2.2)** where it was bolted down through the worktop using lengths of M8 studding. For anyone without such a lifting contraption, 44Kg is

2.1. Top and one side of packing case removed.

more than permitted solo lifting under Health and Safety at Work legislation, but is somewhat less that the old bag of coal or cement. Two people can easily lift it. It may also be noted that the machine is supplied with rubber feet. If these are employed then it is not necessary to bolt the machine down; in which case its location may be easily changed.

Initial impressions

For a machine costing so little, there will

2.2. Lathe has been slid across on to bench to be bolted down.

2.3. Clear indexable dials on cross slide and top slide.

2.5. Checking headstock alignment and chuck runout.

no doubt be design/ production shortcuts but there are also a few unexpected pleasant surprises. Both the crosslide and topslide are fitted with extremely clear indexable dials **(Photo 2.3)**. It was mentioned above that the drive is a variable speed DC system, and that the catalogue quotes a minimum speed of 100rpm. There is also a built in tachometer **(Photo 2.4)** and it was found that in low gear 40rpm was achievable at the lower end of the range. However as this low speed is obtained by motor control (rather than

reduction gears) the transmitted torque will not be massive.

A quick check on headstock alignment was made, using a rough and ready method employing a silver steel bar gripped in the 3-jaw chuck and a clock gauge mounted on the saddle **(Photo 2.5)**. This indicated a small error in the horizontal plane (less than 0.0010 in. over four inches) and nothing measurable in the vertical. This would imply that work held in the chuck and turned nominally parallel would always exhibit a slight taper, of

2.4. Tacho shows spindle speed.

2.6. Set up to check spindle end float.

2.7. Checking tailstock alignment to bed.

2.8. Chuck guard, splash back and gear cover have been removed.

some 0.002in per in. However this inaccuracy is unlikely to cause difficulties since

• It is likely that parts made on the machine will not be long, and

• Where this level of precision is needed, finishing would probably be by filing/lapping.

The same set up was also used to look at the accuracy of the chuck, and here the runout was some 0.0015 in. at one inch from the chuck jaws, so comfortably less than 0.0010 in. eccentricity. Setting a clock to check spindle endfloat **(Photo 2.6)** gave 0.003 in. (applying load with a small lever) but no measurable movement radially. To examine alignment of the tailstock barrel with the bed, the barrel was first extended to the extent of the graduations and clamped. A clock was then set from the toolpost **(Photo 2.7)** and the saddle traversed to move the clock along the extent of the exposed barrel (about 50mm). No measurable deviation was found in either vertical or horizontal planes. Note that this was a check on

alignment of tailstock to bed, not of tailstock to headstock concentricity, which may if necessary be adjusted. It should be noted that ARC do not check or adjust the headstock during preparation, but recommend that this is done by the user once the machine is installed in the final position where it is to be used.

On initially switching on the lathe, at first nothing happened; while I was preparing to decry Chinese quality, the penny dropped that the chuck guard was open, and this is interlocked with the spindle control. Once this was corrected, it sprang into life.

Procedural summary

The following procedure is based on that developed by Arc Euro Trade over several years experience with these lathes. In summary it constitutes a near total stripdown, clean, lubricate, rebuild and adjust. They also modify the leadscrew bearings to facilitate oiling. From my own observation, it seems that the Chinese are extremely generous with the external preservative oil, but not so, where it comes to lubricating hidden parts. Notably, the leadscrew

2.9. Showing the misalignment of the changewheels.

bearings and the apron assembly (gears and bearings) appeared dry. This machine appeared to be coated with a clear, low viscosity preservative, however some are treated with a thicker red concoction, (which ARC jokingly refer to as "Chicken Fat")

The essential strip and build work can be carried out using the supplied toolkit (open-ended spanners and Allen keys) augmented by a couple of Pozi screwdrivers and a 7mm AF spanner. However, for convenience I did in some instances use similar items from my own toolbox. In addition, while the machine is

2.10. Tumbler lever down travel is impeded by contact with the casting. This prevents correct meshing of the smaller white nylon gear.

dismantled, the opportunity may be taken to effect one or two improvements, and here one will require either a fine file or diamond lap, and also access to a drilling machine for the leadscrew bearing mod.

Stripdown

The first components removed are the chuck guard, (two Pozi screws), the splashback (more screws) and the changegear cover (two long Allen screws) **(Photo 2.8).** With the change gears exposed, it is possible to observe the general alignment of the meshing. As can be seen from **Photo 2.9** the gear alignment is out by a couple of mm or so, resulting in incomplete contact across the teeth which could lead to premature wear or even breakage. Two solutions may be considered – a) lightly bend the support plate with a lever or b) add a washer at reassembly to bring the assembly into line. I chose the latter course.

The changewheels are then removed starting with that on the lead screw, followed by removing the support

2.11. Showing clearance between larger white gear and washer. Right; 2.12. After adjusting the motor position, clearance has been gained between the belt and the headstock casting.

plate. Then, looking from the end of the lathe, the tumbler assembly may be checked for correct action and meshing. In this case it can be seen **(Photo 2.10)** that when the tumbler lever is moved to the lower position, contact occurs between part of the lever and a gear carrier casting, and that this prevents correct meshing of the tumbler gear. The solution will be to file away a little material from one or both fouling parts. Once the carrier casting has been detached, the tumbler movement may be rechecked. A second foul is possible between the larger white gear and the washer under the lever retaining screw. **Photo 2.11** shows that in this case, clearance exists. If there is a foul, it may be possible to encourage the washer sideways with a screwdriver on assembly, or to file a small flat on the washer, and carefully align this whilst tightening the screw. The tumbler assembly and alloy belt cover are then removed.

Moving to the rear of the machine, it is then possible to examine the tracking of the motor drive belt. Light contact had been occurring between the belt and the headstock casting. The flanges on the motor pulley determine the belt position, so the remedy is to shift the motor slightly in a direction away from the tailstock. It is pivoted between two Allen screws beneath the bed and the operation is simply a case of slacken both locknuts, then undo one screw and tighten the other. As can be seen from **Photo 2.12** clearance has now been obtained.

The dismantling procedure then continues with removal of tailstock, toolpost and, after slackening the gib screws, the topslide moving section. Undoing the two retaining screws then allows the topslide base to be detached. Similarly, the cross slide components are slackened and removed, leaving the saddle and apron in place. Two Allen screws locate each leadscrew bearing, and removal of the one at the tailstock end can be followed by detachment of the apron. With the clasp nuts open, this can be slid carefully along the leadscrew and

2.13. *The diamond lap has been carved away at an angle to permit access to the root of dovetails.*

2.14. *Raised metal around stamped numbers has been dressed off with lap.*

removed. Before removing the saddle, the six Allen screws on the underside are slackened to give greater clearance. This can then be slid along the bed and off at the tailstock end. All that remains is to take off the second leadscrew bearing and the leadscrew.

Examination and Reassembly

Jingoistic humourists used to comment that Chinese machines were OK if you treated them as a kit of parts. It seems there is still an element of truth in that view, at least as regards the "Factory Assembled" condition. It must be acknowledged that the manufacture is being undertaken using decent production equipment, so the inherent component quality is good. It would appear, however that the assembly process does not benefit from the same care and attention that one comes to expect from say, a Myford. This element of care and attention can though be introduced by the new owner, who has a certain level of mechanical or engineering skill, and or is prepared to spend some time to read through various

articles on this subject, as suggested earlier.

Apart from the notes above, the principal points of criticism relate to the cross and topslide, where for each pair of sliding surfaces, one is typically finely ground while the other is milled, showing significant machining marks. Here is where the traditional skilled machine tool fitter would scrape the slides to improve accuracy and smoothness. I do not class myself as having anywhere near the required level of skill for this, so simply gave the milled surfaces a gentle rub with a fine triangular file and a small diamond lap. The lap has been modified by trimming away the plastic backing at an angle to allow it to sit fully into the corners of the dovetails **(Photo 2.13).**

The first area to be dealt with is the underside of the bed. The upper surface and vee way are ground all over, but the sides (which make no contact) and underside appear to be milled albeit with good finish. The diamond lap was carefully held against the underside and drawn

2.15. Underside view of saddle shows "push-pull" adjustment screws.

along several times using light pressure. This would remove any local high spots. A small area on the top surface of the bed was also given the lap treatment at this point. The serial number is stamped into the upper working surface after grinding and this causes metal to be raised around the edges of the numerals. Taking the raised material off with the lap, left the number still easily legible **(Photo 2.14)** and improved the sliding action over this area. (Unlikely to be used at the very end of the bed, but model engineers are notorious

for stretching machine capacity so you never know.) The lower working surfaces of the saddle were then coated with "Copaslip" (Arc use this) and the casting slid back on to the bed.

It may be useful at this point to add a brief description of the adjustment arrangement. Two metal strips are pulled up to the underside by three Allen screws, relative thicknesses of bed and saddle being chosen so that pulling up tight would clamp to the bed. Jacking screws with locknuts are also fitted and these function to push the strips downwards and set a working clearance. The arrangement may be seen in **Photo 2.15**. Thus the adjustment sequence is a repetitive process of lightly adjusting the opposed push - pull actions to achieve good fit and feel. It should be noted that firm tightening of the pull up screws is not required and in fact if overdone (according to web notes) may actually cause fracture of the strips.

Attention then moves to the apron, leadscrew and associated bearings. Here, Arc drill an oilway and add internal oil grooves. Many owners may choose not to make this change and rely on oiling from the bearing ends, however it probably will result in extended life. While it would be possible do the drilling on the C3 using the milling attachment, as the lathe was in pieces, the simpler alternative was to use the VMC mill. **Photo 2.16** shows the RH bearing gripped in the vice canted up 45 degrees and a piece of thin sheet brass used under the point of the drill to get close to the centre of the curved surface. (When the brass was horizontal, the drill was close to centre.) The bearing length is

2.16. The RH leadscrew bearing being set up for drilling an oilway.

2.17. Inside view of the apron showing the half nuts and gears.

2.18. Milled surface of the cross slide dovetail is lightly rubbed with the lap.

20mm so the hole was drilled 10mm from one end.

Following the Arc example, a Minicraft drill with a small burr, was then employed to cut a diagonal oilway within the bearing. The 45 degree cant mentioned would ensure that the oil hole would be conveniently accessible after assembly. A similar series of operations was carried out on the LH bearing.

Attention was then given to the apron assembly. The half nuts were removed, and their respective dovetails given a touch with the lap. These, the shafts and the gears were reassembled with more Copaslip **(Photo 2.17).** With the bearings and leadscrew also given a dose of Copaslip, the LH bearing with leadscrew could be jury-rigged. The apron (with clasp nuts open) was then carefully threaded over the leadscrew and loosely attached to the saddle. After fitting the RH leadscrew bearing, the screws holding the LH were tightened, whilst pressing the bearing towards the right. Similarly, the RH bearing was nipped up whilst applying pressure towards the left. (The reason is that the leadscrew endfloat is set by the

relative positions of the two bearings and this sequence aims to minimise this.)

Now the saddle and apron are moved as far as possible towards the right hand end of the bed. The half nuts are then closed, and the two bolts securing the saddle to the apron are progressively tightened. (The securing bolts pass through elongated holes and this procedure sets the apron position correctly in relation to the leadscrew.) As a final check in this area, with the half nuts still closed, the RH leadscrew bearing bolts may be slackened and retightened, again pushing to the left. This will allow it to move up or down a few thou to centralise the leadscrew on the half nuts.

Apparently it is not unknown for the rack position to be less than perfect, resulting in poor meshing of the carriage gear teeth. If necessary the rack may need repositioning for optimum engagement.

The lap was again brought into play for the cross slide and top slide dovetail surfaces – just a gentle rub to clear any high spots **(Photo 2.18).** The cross slide with its lead screw, bearing and handle were then added again with a measure of

2.19. Showing the step filed to ensure correct movement of the tumbler assembly.

2.20: The tumbler bracket is a pressing with sharp edges on one face.

Copaslip lubricant. The gibs on these slides are relatively thick (about 4mm) and adjustment is by socket head grub screws and locknuts. These screws have dog points, which locate closely in drilled recesses in the gibs. It was found that there was some reluctance to re engage with the recesses, and so the screws were each given a very light chamfer on the dog

point. (Out of interest, G H Thomas recommended that gibs are pinned, and it may be argued that this arrangement gives much the same effect. When rotating the topslide, a notable clunk could be felt (and heard). This turned out to be another case of metal raised by stamping (after grinding); in this case the fiducial mark for angle setting. Once again, a few strokes with the lap effected a cure.

The alloy belt cover was then refitted. Before adding the tumbler bracket, a small amount of metal was filed away from the foul point mentioned above. The tumbler was then fitted, ensuring that clearance existed between the nylon gear and washer mentioned earlier and shown in **Photo 2.11**. Metal was also removed from the cast carrier **(Photo 2.19)** which was then refitted along with the associated gears after lubricating the bearings. Examination of the changewheel bracket showed this to be a pressing, **(Photo 2.20)** with sharp edges on one side. These were dressed off with a file before the bracket with wheels was

2.21: The gear alignment has been improved by the addition of a washer.

2.22. Shows the burr raised by the tailstock handwheel grubscrew.

2.23. Grubscrew on carriage handwheel has drilled recess.

added, after locating a single washer behind, which would bring the gears into better alignment **(Photo 2.21)** .

The tailstock upper and lower sections were not separated at this stage, however the barrel and screw were removed for lubrication. While this was in pieces, the opportunity was taken to lightly chamfer the end of the barrel, removing a sharpish edge. It was also noted that the handwheel is retained by a cup point grubscrew, which had marked the shaft **(Photo 2.22).** The marking was dressed away with a fine file, and a small brass disc inserted below the screw. In contrast, the carriage handwheel is held by a cone point screw and in this instance, the point locates in a drilled recess **(Photo 2.23).**

Fitting the changewheel cover,

splashback and chuckguard completed the exercise after which the machine was fired up, **(Photo 2.24)** running the saddle under power feed backwards and forwards several times to check operation. Operating the various slides manually was now noticeably smoother compared to the earlier, as received "Factory assembled" condition.

Whilst this was my experience of the "Factory assembled" model, I understand that Arc's in house preparation process may find other "variables" which may need to be looked at. Any that do arise will be covered on Arc's website in due course, under their projects and articles section.

In the next chapter, we will examine the basic equipment needed to work with the machine and some of the accessories, which are available for it.

2.24. Assembled and under power.

Chapter 3

Tooling Materials and Geometry

Given that many Mini Lathes will be purchased by enthusiasts with little metalworking experience, this chapter aims to give basic advice on the action, geometry, and materials for cutting tools.

Nowadays, sets of carbide tipped tools are available at such low prices that this is often the chosen initial route forwards. However situations can arise when something a little non-standard is called for, and here the following notes may be of help.

Although primarily a metalworking machine, no doubt many owners will put theirs to use on other materials such as wood, plastic, MDF, etc, and these activities may require tooling a little different to the normal off the shelf items. Some of the examples, which are illustrated, relate to large turning and milling applications, however the general concepts are equally applicable to smaller scale work.

Materials

Before looking at some particular examples, it may be worth considering some of the materials at our disposal, and the general action of cutting. The phrase "like a knife through butter" comes to mind, and if a knife blade is held vertically then drawn horizontally and sideways across a block of butter, as in **Photo 3.1**, producing a thin curl of yellow "edible swarf" then the action is very similar to that occuring in metal cutting. In any cutting situation, the tool must be harder than the work. In addition, frictional heat is created and if the temperature is allowed to rise too high, then the tool will soften and lose its edge. The temperature achieved will depend on a number of factors including the workpiece material, and the speed of cutting. While no one wants to waste time machining, we are not so completely bound by the "time is money" mantra as our

3.1. Drawing a knife across butter simulates a typical cutting action

3.2. Two "D" bits mild steel on right for MDF, hard silver steel on left for metalcutting.

3.3. Mild steel cutters to finish aluminium valve seats.

industrial counterparts. Doing things more slowly can remove the need for exotic tooling.

Nowadays we tend to think almost exclusively in terms of tooling having either High Speed Steel (HSS) or tungsten carbide (TCT) cutting edges. However, bearing in mind that wood could cut butter, it is sometimes useful to remember that provided the tool is harder than the work, lower tech solutions may be useful. HSS and carbide make excellent hard wearing tools, but they arrive in the hardened state, and therefore any carving to shape must be done with a grind wheel – green grit or diamond in the case of carbide. Other materials worthy of consideration for particular circumstances include mild steel, silver steel, gauge plate, and high tensile bolts or Allen screws.

Mild steel (and even brass)

At first sight this sounds like sheer stupidity, but for a fast way to produce a tool to do the odd job on soft materials such as

medium density fibreboard (MDF), it does actually work. It is also readily available in a wide range of shapes and sizes, also much cheaper than silver steel. **Photo 3.2** includes a "D" bit in mild steel, which was turned, sawn and filed quickly to shape for a job on the mill. It might also be accommodated in the tailstock. The memory is fading a little, but it may have been to make an MDF part to assist in marking out a car gearbox adapter plate. For short runs, mild steel may also be used on plastics, although, it may often be almost as easy to upgrade to carbon steel/silver steel or perhaps gauge plate. **Photo 3.3** shows a pair of valve seat finishing cutters made by Loctiting mild steel cutting parts to silver steel stems. This may sound a bit back to front in terms of material selection but for truing up the seats in a small aluminium cylinder head, they worked. The silver steel gave accurate location in the valve guides, and the mild steel was sufficiently hard to gently scrape the seats. Now that the format has been proved, next time I'll make a

3.4 Toolmakers reamers from silver steel.

set in silver steel for longer life.

Silver steel or carbon steel

As with mild steel, these are supplied in soft condition, and thus can be readily filed or sawn to shape. It may be as a result of slight wear, but my regular (possibly slightly worn) 0.250in. reamer produces holes, which are just too tight for silver steel rods. My solution was to make a toolmakers reamer **(Photo 3.4)** from a length of the same batch of silver steel to take out the last thou or so and ensure a perfect fit. Tools made from these materials may be hardened by heating to "cherry red" then quenching in water. Tubal Cain, in his excellent book "Hardening, Tempering & Heat Treatment" *(Workshop Practice Series*, Number 1) suggests 770 - 790 Degrees C. heating slowly and holding at temperature for one hour per inch of thickness. This may be followed by tempering to improve resistance to shock (and reduce hardness) but I have to confess that I usually leave things hard. A quick and dirty test that acceptable

3.5 Commercial cutter is easily replicated in more robust form.

hardness has been achieved is to try to file the tool. The file should just skate over the surface. Final light grinding will then produce a keen edge. Silver steel is most readily available in ground bar form in a variety of diameters and is therefore ideal for situations calling for round bits.

Gauge plate

Otherwise known as precision ground oil hardening flat stock, this is alloy steel whose composition will probably vary a little depending on the manufacturer, but will typically include carbon, chrome, tungsten and vanadium as constituents. It is readily available in a wide variety of flat sections. The J&L Industrial Supply catalogue lists thicknesses from 1/32in. to 2in. and widths ranging from 3/8in. to 12in. In addition squares from 1/8in. to 2in. are also shown, as are metric sections. Lengths are typically 18in. or 500mm. Like silver steel, this is supplied in the soft state, and hence is easy to cut and shape. I have found it to be particularly useful for form tools (lathe) and for providing the hard face

Above: 3.6. Quenching in water may cause severe cracking. Right: 3.7. High tensile bolts provide the source material for keyway cutter (left and internal grooving tool (right).

for dies (punching).

Photo 3.5 shows a cheap commercial woodworking bit which has several interchangeable blades, intended for cutting holes for hinges in kitchen units. The same principle was applied to a home made heavier duty version for work on plastic jigs for chrome plating. This employed 0.187in. thick gauge plate for the blade, and featured a 5/8in. diameter shank threaded to fit a Clarkson milling collet chuck.

Heat treatment is quite straightforward, and detailed on the packaging, viz. heat to 780-800 degrees C. holding for one hour per inch of thickness then quench in oil. Purists will disagree but I have successfully used old engine oil. Just make sure the container holds plenty of oil so that it does not get too hot, and have a metal cover handy just in case you need to quell flaming surface vapour. Obviously this is better done outdoors. Note that the manufacturers call for quenching in oil. I have tried quenching in water, and while sometimes successful,

Photo 3.6 shows that disaster can ensue, here an obvious crack in a square punch, due to the use of water. Manufacturers packing also details tempering temperatures and resultant hardness levels.

High tensile bolts

These, and particularly Allen screws of known provenance are made from a quality alloy steel. As supplied it can, like mild and carbon steels be readily carved to shape using conventional tooling. It will then in general respond adequately to a rough and ready heat to about 800 degrees C followed by quenching in water or oil. By making use of the fact that the head diameter is somewhat larger than that of the stem, Bolts can be turned into useful tools for boring or internal grooving (**Photo 3.7**). According to one web site I chanced upon, non HT bolts use the same steel, but are not heat-treated.

High speed steel

Until the advent of carbide, this was the material pretty well universally adopted for

3.8. Old taps are another source of HSS in various diameters.

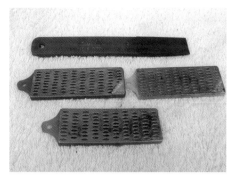

3.10. Four diamond hones or laps.

industrial tooling. It was developed to allow faster machining speeds than were possible with carbon steel as this metal retains its hardness at higher temperatures. Its heat treatment is considered outside the scope of the amateur shop. It is sourced in the hard - ready to use - condition, and hence cannot be sawn or filed. It can of course be cut with an abrasive disc and ground to shape or sharpened using a normal grinding wheel.

It may be purchased as square section tool bits e.g. for our purposes probably 3/16in. or 1/4in. section by about three or four inches in length. The quickest way to cut to length may be to grind a notch then apply a bending load with vice and pliers. (safety glasses recommended) It may also be supplied in the form of drill rod in a range of diameters.

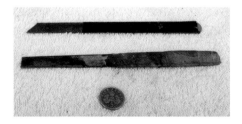

Also bear in mind that your worn out drills are likely to be HSS as are many taps, and if like me you tend to hoard these **(Photo 3.8)** then a ready supply of tool tips is to hand. These may be located in holders fashioned for specific duties. Hacksaw blades may be carbon steel, high speed steel or bi-metallic - a HSS edge welded to a flexible back.

Tungsten carbide

Carbide was the next big thing in industrial tooling which permitted a step change in machining speeds from HSS (often up by some 300 per cent) being harder and more temperature resistant than HSS. Sharpening and shaping carbide can be achieved with a green grit wheel, however my experience is that this gives a course finish to the tool and a significant improvement is obtained if the edge is finished with a diamond wheel or hone. A selection of cheap diamond hones is shown in **Photo 3.10**, and note that the

3.9. Broken or blunt hacksaw blades used here as knives, may also be used for grooving.

3.11. Cutters from JB. Use until worn then turn into tips.

3.12. Triangular and part off tips discarded by an industrial user.

non-perforated version is a bit more expensive but very much easier when sharpening small edges. Diamond wheels are available from a number of suppliers in the UK such as Eternal Tools and Arc Euro Trade.

Solid carbide tooling has been available from industrial suppliers for some time, but the costs make one think twice for hobby use. However items such as carbide end mills and burrs are frequently available from J B Cutting Tools **(Photo 3.11)** and their stand is well worth a visit at shows. These tools can be used until blunt then either sharpened or allowed to become raw material for new tools. Indexable tips **(Photo 3.12)**

discarded by industrial users can also be worth looking at. Re-sharpening would be a non-starter for factory work, but can work in our favour. Carbide is also available from specialist suppliers in forms such as round, half round, square and triangular rod. I don't recall where it came from, but did acquire a few pieces **(Photo 3.13)** at a factory sale some years ago. Cutting/breaking follows the same line as for HSS, but a diamond wheel is suggested. **Photo 3.14** shows a piece of heavy-duty woodworking bandsaw blade. A two foot length of this carries twenty or so teeth each of which has a brazed on carbide tip. Also shown in the picture is a transverse slice with one tip, which is destined for

3.13. Carbide in a variety of forms.

3.14. A transverse slice has been cut from this bandsaw blade.

use in grooving or part off applications.

Tool geometry

One of the over simplifications I remember from many years ago was the "sixty degree" principle. The idea was that you could approximate the cutting tool edge to sixty degrees. For many applications it does work. For a typical right hand lathe tool, as shown in **Fig 3.1**, if you start with a square 90 degrees, then take off say 10 for side clearance and 15 for top rake you are left with 65, not far off the 60. In a similar manner if a section were to be taken part way across a drill lip, the angle between the face of the spiral flute and the clearance surface at the end of the drill would again be not far off the same figure. If we think back to the knife - butter analogy, and instead of a knife, draw a triangular section scraper across the surface, then, provided the lower surface has a clearance angle, and does not skate over the butter, then again a yellow curl results.

Virtually all metal cutting operations rely on a selection of suitable angles - rake, clearance and relief, the relevant nomenclature being given in **Fig 3.1**. Clearance is needed as with the butter analogy to ensure that the tool does not skid, and the edge is allowed to cut. Much of the time this is fairly self evident, however, careful thought may be needed in such applications as very coarse threads. One of the tools shown in **Photo**

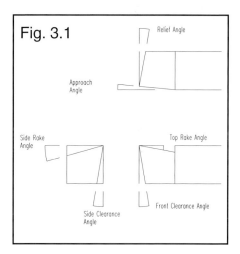

Fig. 3.1

Relief Angle

Approach Angle

Side Rake Angle

Top Rake Angle

Side Clearance Angle

Front Clearance Angle

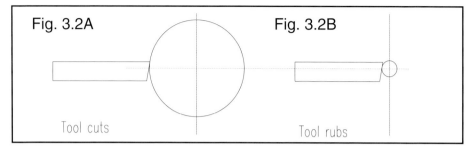

Fig. 3.2A   Fig. 3.2B

Tool cuts   Tool rubs

3.15 was set up to cut an internal spiral groove. Because of the extreme change gear ratio, the lathe was actually driven by hand using the lead screw handle. In fact the tip was set over around 45 degrees to achieve the correct angle. The rake angle will tend to be higher for soft materials such as aluminium, although a zero figure is needed for brass to avoid snatching and digging in. With no relief angle, the length of cutting edge would increase as the tool is fed in, leading to excessive cutting forces, however the existence of this feature also means that a turned diameter actually looks like a very fine screw thread when examined under powerful magnification. Adding a small radius to the tool tip tends to improve the surface finish.

It is probably worth mentioning one or two situations where the lack of clearance may arise. If an external turning tool is set just a little too high, then all will be well until the work diameter reduces to the point where contact occurs below the cutting edge. At that point the tool mysteriously stops cutting and the tyro is tempted to apply more force. **Figs 3.2 A** and **B** illustrate this situation. Another non-clearance situation may arise when cutting a coarse or multi start thread. Although a tool may appear to have adequate front clearance it is worth double-checking.

For an internal tool, the situation is reversed, and it may be found that mounting a boring tool slightly above centre will permit the use of one a little deeper and more robust. Downwards deflection of an above centre boring tool will tend to reduce the depth of cut and hence tendency to chatter. A point to watch is that if taken to extremes then the feed is not truly radial, and increases in bore size will deviate from the amounts indicated by the cross slide dial.

Having touched on the consequences of incorrect tool height, we should now mention form tools. These are often made to produce multiple features in one feed movement. By their nature they usually have a cutting edge which extends over a

3.15. Boring bars and internal threading tools using clamped HSS bits.

range of radii. Thus if it has significant rake on its top surface, then part of the edge will deviate from the ideal height. Hence form tools are often made with zero top rake, so that the whole cutting edge will be on centreline.

Rake angles were also mentioned above. Although much has been written on optimum angles for particular materials, my impression is that these are generally not critical. Provided a tool has clearance and a sharp edge, it will cut, although it probably will not deliver ideal performance and the best possible finish. Note however that for brass, zero rake is recommended to stop tools snatching and grabbing.

Feed, speed, and depth of cut

It was noted earlier that heat is generated during cutting, dependant on, amongst other parameters, the surface speed of cutting, which, for a given spindle speed will rise in proportion to the diameter of the work. The limiting factor here for tool materials is the temperature at which they start to soften. Thus carbon steel must be operated more slowly than high-speed steel, and it in turn, more slowly than tungsten carbide. By the same token, in general, work made from softer or less tough raw material may be cut faster than harder counterparts, using the same tool material.

Let us now consider a typical right hand knife turning tool, which is normally used for turning plain diameters and for facing the end of the work. **Fig 3.3** depicts such a tool in operation. For our purposes, the feed will be the amount by which the tool advances for each revolution of the work – in essence like a very fine screw thread. While the depth of cut will be the amount by which the tool has been moved

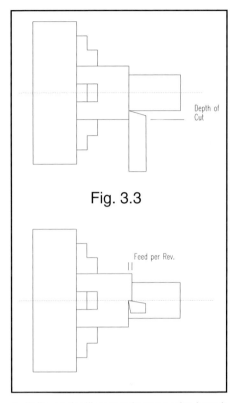

Fig. 3.3

radially, and will approximate to the length of cutting edge engaged. (In the case of a facing operation, the depth of cut will be measured along the axis, and the feed per rev. measured radially.)

Larger industrial lathes usually enjoy two independent mechanisms for traversing the saddle, one for fine feed, and a leadscrew for screwcutting. Small machines intended for amateur use, such as the Mini Lathe and larger Myford Seven, often have only the leadscrew, so that it is then necessary to set up an arrangement of changewheels to achieve the desired feed per rev. When using a small lathe, my

3.16. Toolholder from one inch square stock to take carbide insert.

3.17. Small boring bars, tips are brazed in carbide rod.

own preference is to use the leadscrew for screwcutting only, and to apply the feed manually for all other work. This approach has several benefits. First the condition and accuracy of the leadscrew is better preserved for a longer life. Second, the hands on style gives an immediate feel for what the machine is doing and how the cut is progressing. You are then able to react instantly in the case of chatter or overload, and reduce accordingly.

Examples from the toolbox
Turning tools

Photo 3.16 shows a heavy duty holder made from one-inch square black steel bar. A recess has been milled to take one of the large triangular inserts shown in **Photo 3.12**. Location is fixed by a) the rear edge of the recess, b) a spring dowel driven in, and c) a clamp acting on the top surface. It was intended for use in a Herbert 2D capstan lathe to form i.c. engine valve blanks from 5/8in dia. stainless steel. These were produced in one pass to a tolerance of just over 0.0010, and the nose radius and edge angle formed the

underside of the head in the same operation.

Boring bars for smallish diameters were something I got to grips with very early on. **Photo 3.15** showed a selection of holders fitted with HSS round section tips, typically about 1/8in. diameter. These and their close cousins having brazed in carbide rod **(Photo 3.17)** were made in the late 1970's, and as can be seen by the amount of tip protruding are in some cases nearing the end of useful life. One more recent addition features a part off tip working from the inside out. I chose to make the shanks from 1/2in. diameter mild steel, and locate in a block of square section, drilled through 1/2in. Nowadays, the block tends to be redundant as the tools are accommodated in quick-change holders having a vee groove. Note that if the tip is held by a clamp screw then it may be adjusted for optimum cutting/ clearance angles, whereas if the tip is brazed, then the counter advantage is that it is easier to locate it at the end of the bar allowing boring to the base of blind holes.

For occasions where a sizeable hole

3.18. Fabricated trepanning tool with brazed in part off tip.

3.19. J & S toolholder takes 3/16in. square HSS toolbit.

is needed through a modest thickness, (say up to a half inch) one way to avoid masses of swarf is to employ a trepanning tool. This is a bit like a single tooth hole saw. For cutting holes around the two inch diameter mark, I fabricated the one shown in **Photo 3.18**. A half-inch diameter shank is welded to a disk, and this in turn to a short length of 2in. diameter 1/8in. thick steel tube. A slot is cut in the tube to take a parting off tip, which is than brazed in. The tube gives good support to the carbide tip

and automatically gives the necessary clearance.

High speed steel toolbits used to be employed regularly in industry, often being housed in holders such as that made by Jones and Shipman and shown in **Photo 3.19**. The advantage of such holders was that they presented the tip at a compound angle so the top surface did not require grinding. These industrial holders tend to be somewhat on the large side for our applications, but the tips may be held in a

3.20. Home made block presents toolbit at compound angle.

3.21. End on view of block showing angle.

3.22. Home made holder for 5/16in. Eclipse part off blade.

3.23. Section sawn from large holder to be welded to smaller .

home made block, as illustrated in **Photos 3.20 and 3.21**. A groove has been milled using angle settings in two planes to cant the top surface backwards and sideways. Grinding the tool and subsequent sharpening is thus constrained to two surfaces. Shanks of old taps may be held in a similar holder, which is simply drilled through at an angle then split.

The price of part off holders has plummeted over the last decade as imports from India and China have become available. **Photo 3.22** shows a home brewed version fabricated in earlier years to take a standard 5/16in. Eclipse blade. A variation on the theme could take a piece of

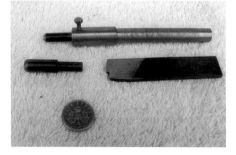

Photo 3.23 shows an item of work in progress. I wanted to be able to use standard diamond shaped carbide tips, and the holders for these are generally available only in sections too large to fit in my small QC holders. The end has been cut from a large commercial holder and will be welded or brazed to a smaller half inch square shank

Mention was made earlier of form tools. **Photo 3.24** shows a tool made from gauge plate to form small spheres. For the application intended, it was unsuccessful because the components fractured due to stem geometry. However it is likely that this approach would work well if making parts such as small handrail knobs especially in brass. The other tools in the same picture are of sharpened hollow tubes in hard silver steel used to finish small spheres.

Coventry die heads have become less popular, and thus their cutters **(Photo 3.25)** may be found available cheaply. These can

3.24. Gauge plate form tool and sharp tube tools for finishing spheres.

3.25. Cutter blade from Coventry die head.

3.26. Above - tapered D bit, below - one to produce 60deg countersink.

then be clamped to holders.

Milling and drilling tools

D bits are well known to model engineers. **Photo 3.2** showed a couple, one in mild steel for short-term use on MDF, the other in hard silver steel for producing a flat-bottomed hole in a mild steel component. The general principle can also be extended to other applications. **Photo 3.26** shows a couple of examples. The larger was produced to cut a revised taper in a racing car steering arm. As can be seen quenching in water caused cracking, but a satisfactory taper was cut. Spade drills seem to receive little attention for application to metalwork, although they are well known in woodworking circles. The selection shown in **Photo 3.27** came to me from a friend of the family who ran a university departmental workshop. They may have been intended for work on wood or plastics, but I have tried the 1/4in. version on aluminium with good results. **Photo 3.28** shows a carbide tipped twist drill from the well known manufacturer Guhring. The tip is a piece of flat carbide inserted into the tip and brazed in. So the tip geometry is really very similar to a spade drill but the shank has spiral flutes to aid chip removal. Spade drills may offer

3.27. A selection of spade drills ranging from 0.25in. down to 0.030in.

3.28. Carbide drill tip from Guhring is similar to spade.

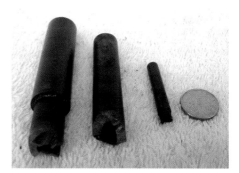

3.29. Hollow or shell milling cutters made from silver steel.

an easy way of making undersize drills for interference fits.

The detail of the Guhring drill also prompts an easy route to carbide tipped drills. A standard masonry drill is fitted with a similar tip, but if you examine the cutting edges you will find that for drilling stone they are not sharp but chamfered. It is an easy matter to regrind to a sharp edge for work on metal. This produces a tool geometrically similar to the Guhring example but at much reduced cost. The result, though, is unlikely to be as good as say a solid carbide drill such as is now available from suppliers such as Chronos, as the grade of carbide may be incorrect for the new application.

Work on items such as i.c. engine cylinder heads with integral valve guides, may dictate a need for a hollow or shell type cutter. **Photo 3.29** shows a couple of these. It was interesting to note that after one tooth broke away, the cutting performance seemed to improve.

Chapter 4

Getting Started- Tooling Up

In this chapter, we commence by considering those additional items that the beginner will need in order to get going, then move on to some basic turning.

Turning

Before starting to do any turning work on the machine, it may be worth (for the benefit of novices) reviewing some of the associated bits and pieces that will be needed. First and foremost, a lathe cannot cut metal without tools, and here, you may choose to follow the traditional route and buy high speed steel tool bits, which you then need to grind to shape. Our regular tooling suppliers offer a bewildering array of lathe tools ranging from basic lengths of high speed steel, through brazed tip tools (HSS and carbide) to replaceable tipped tools. Arc Euro Trade offer two sets of tooling associated with this lathe, the first being two holders with HSS and carbide matching bits as shown in **Photo 4.1.** Alternatively, you may choose to purchase a set of carbide tipped tools such as that illustrated in **Photo 4. 2**. This set is comprised of eleven tools and actually costs a little less than the kit in **Photo 4.1**. Given that the price for the set is considerably under what you might pay for a single industrial tool holder this looks to be a sensible way forwards.

4.1 Tooling set – two holders plus toolbits in HSS and carbide .

4.2 Set of eleven carbide tipped turning tools .

4.3 Low cost double ended bench grinder – note the guards and rests have been removed.

4.4 Set of four diamond laps from Arc (colours denote roughness grade .

Sharpening

Tools need to be sharpened, and here the usual solution is one of the many double-ended bench grinders sold by the DIY shops. I use the one shown in **Photo 4.3.** Note that this is now destined for a specific non-standard duty, and has been robbed of its work rests and guards. Normally these grinders come with grey grit wheels, which are suitable for sharpening steel but not carbide. Carbide needs either a "green grit" or a diamond wheel. However for just touching up the edge on a tool, it is usually possible to work with one of the low cost plastic backed diamond laps **(Photo 4.4)**. If you choose to start off with a set of carbide tools such as **Photo 4.2**, and buying a grinder is to be put back, then one of these would suffice as a first step. Diamond laps are available in two basic forms - perforated and unperforated backing. The perforated variety is fine for work on flat surfaces, but the unperforated ones are better for work on the tips of tools. They are also supplied in a range of grit sizes.

Drilling

In order to create a hole, you will need some form of drill. In addition, holes need to be started, usually with a centre drill. For our purposes, these come in a range of sizes – Imperial BS 1 to BS 4 and metric body diameters 4mm to 10mm. They are also supplied to cut two forms of centre – plain 60 degree, and bell which unsurprisingly drills a bellmouth shaped hole. Components made on the Mini lathe are likely to be small, so my suggestion would be to acquire a couple of the smaller sizes. The body and pilot diameters of the BS1 and BS3 are 1/8in. / 3/64in. and 1/4in. / 7/64in. respectively. **Photo 4.5** shows a couple of typical centre drills.

Back in the 1970's when I first took up model engineering, I was fortunate to be given a two sets of number drills 1 to 60 (5.8mm to 1mm) and 61 to 80 (1mm to 0.35mm) and also a set of imperial drills 1/16 to 1/2in by 1/64in increments. These were later augmented by a set of metric. Such sets are still available, but with the inevitable movement towards metrication, nowadays, I would recommend that the novice start off with one set of metric drills, namely 1mm to 6mm by 0.1mm

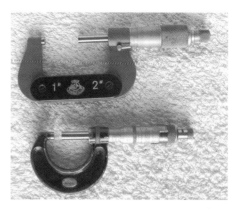

4.5 Two typical centre drills. Right: 4.6 Imperial micrometers – 0 to 1in. and 1 to 2 in..

increments. These are available as a boxed set from many of our regular suppliers such as Chronos, Tracy Tools, Arc, Warco, etc. Further acquisitions would be determined by the direction of personal model making interest, and might include the smaller number drills to No.80, or a range extending upwards to perhaps 10 or 13mm or even larger.

Measuring

If you go back in history, it was often claimed that much accurate work was done using nothing more complicated than a good quality six-inch rule. Graduations would be to 64ths, so with good eyesight, measurements could be to better than 0.0015in. Engineering shops would typically have a selection of micrometers, **(Photo 4.6)** vernier (later digital) callipers, **(Photo 4.7)** and perhaps slip gauges **(Photo 4.8)**. Over the years, the cost of precision measuring equipment has kept coming down, so that today it is possible to buy a 6in. digital calliper for less than ten pounds.

My suggestion would be for the novice to start with one of the cheap Chinese

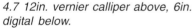

4.7 12in. vernier calliper above, 6in. digital below.

4.8 Set of slip gauges

4.9 Optional 4-jaw chuck chuck supplied for the Mini Lathe.

4.10 Optional faceplate .

digital callipers, as for a modest outlay this will give outside/inside measurement coupled with imperial/metric conversion. My own preference is to work with micrometers for sizes up to two inches, probably because I have used these far longer than callipers and therefore am better used to the feel. However if you start with callipers, you may conclude that you have no need of a micrometer.

Accessories - workholding and toolholding

The C3 from Arc Euro Trade is supplied as standard, with a three jaw 80mm chuck, a

tailstock MT2 dead centre, change gear set, oil tray and tool kit. This chuck is fine, but for work which is neither round nor hexagonal, either the optional 4-jaw chuck **(Photo 4.9)** or face plate **(Photo 4.10)** would be needed. My own experience suggests that the 4 jaw would see more frequent use than a faceplate and hence be placed higher on the purchasing priority list. (some enthusiasts prefer to use a 4 jaw rather than the 3 jaw as when using it, the concentricity can always be set as accurately as you take time to achieve.)

Some means will be required to hold drills in the tailstock, and for this size of machine I would initially go for a chuck with a range of up to say 10mm such as that supplied by Arc and shown in the lower part of **Photo 4.11**. If your funds will stretch, then you may wish to consider a keyless chuck as an alternative. The upper section

4.11 Two drill chucks with MT2 arbors – above keyless from Albrecht, below keyed type supplied for use with the Mini Lathe.

4.12 Four way toolpost supplied as standard with the C3.

4.13 Optional two way boat type toolpost
.

of **Photo 4.11** shows an Albrecht keyless having a capacity of 10mm. These chucks offer added convenience in that you are not constantly searching for that elusive chuck key, and taking time to apply it. There are however two downsides; the first is price, and the second is size. As can be seen, the keyless is somewhat larger for similar capacity, and on occasions can get in the way of working. It may also be noted that the arbor supplied by Arc features an M10 thread for a drawbar (for milling duties). To keep this thread clean I have added an M10 grubscrew to blank off the end.

The standard C3 toolpost **(Photo 4.12)** is a four way model operating on a built in ratchet system, and is in a sense, a miniaturised version of the arrangement typically found on many larger capstan and centre lathes. Operation is by slackening the handle to allow the post to be rotated anticlockwise just past the next tool position, then back to lock against the

ratchet at one of four 90 degree positions. There are two diametrically opposed schools of thought on the subject of four way posts. For one, they offer a simple method of having up to four tools correctly set and ready for work. For the other they present three unnecessary sharp edges ready to slice into the careless hand.

Arc offer two other toolpost options, the boat type **(Photo 4.13)** and the Quick Change System, which was not available to be photographed at the time of writing.

Brief digression (1)

Old hands will be well aware of the need (apart from special situations) to have lathe tools mounted so that the tool tip operates at centre height. For the benefit of newcomers, if a tool is mounted above centre, then as work moves to a smaller diameter, the tool runs out of clearance and rubs. Conversely, if mounted below centre, then when taking a facing cut, the tool passes across below centre, and

4.14 With tool below centre, facing cut leaves pip.

leaves an uncut area. **Photo 4.14** serves to illustrate these conditions. Hence some form of tool height gauge is worth constructing and that shown in **Photo 4.15** is my quickie solution which uses the top of the cross slide as a height datum.
The components are:

• Three pieces of steel flat bar in this case 20mm x 8mm section cut to lengths 65mm;

4.16 Measure from cross slide over top of bar .

25mm; 20mm. (The section was scientifically determined by what was immediately to hand. You might equally use anything between 6 and 12mm thick for the base, and 3mm thick for the levels.)
• One length of M6 mild steel screwed rod approx 75mm long
• Two M6 nuts
The base is drilled and tapped M6, the rod is screwed in (not protruding below) and retained with Loctite, the remaining parts are drilled 6mm dia. then loaded from the top and adjusted for height between the two nuts.
The lathe centre height can be checked by:
• Take a short length of bar and measure its diameter (D)

4.15 Simple height gauge.

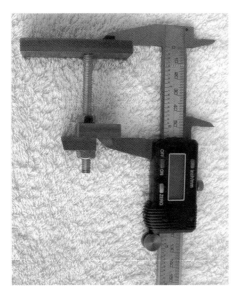

4.17 Adjust the gauge to the calculated dimension .

4.18 When tool is correctly adjusted, work is faced with no pip.

- *Measure the height from the cross slide to the top of the bar (H)**(Photo 4.16)***
- *Rotate the chuck 180 degrees*
- *Measure again the height from cross slide to top of bar (h)*
- *Calculate the average measurement: (H + h) /2*
- *Deduct half the bar diameter (D/2)*
- *Centre height to cross slide is: (H+h)/2 – D/2 or (H+h-D)/2*

The tool height gauge may then be adjusted to and checked against this height as in **Photo 4.17**. Note when using this gauge on the Mini lathe, it is necessary to avoid contact with one of the cross slide nut adjustment/retaining screws which may protrude up from the cross slide surface.

Working with the four-way toolpost version requires the operator to raise each tool with a shim pack to bring the cutting edge to centre height. Shims may be made from strips of metal of varying thicknesses up to say 1/16in or 1.5mm. For fine adjustment, strips cut from aluminium cans, will be found to be about 0.003in thick. Similar useful material may also be salvaged from some of the disposable aluminium cooking trays. **Photo 4.18** shows the result of re facing the part shown earlier in **Photo 14**, but now with the tool set on centre, there is no residual pip.

The boat type toolpost requires no shim packing. Movement of the "boat" in its curved recess allows the nose of the tool to be raised or lowered under the control of the two clamping screws. As this causes some change in tool angle, there is likely to be slight variation in cutting tool

4.19 Plate below carriage stop has moved out of line.

4.20 Drilling 1/8in. diameter hole.

angle compared to the ideal. However this is not of great magnitude, and does not generally cause problems. It may also be observed that Myford has used a similar system successfully for many years.

Saddle/carriage stop

Opinions may differ, but nowadays, I would regard some form of saddle stop as essential, so that cuts up to a shoulder can be made to a repeatable length. Back in the 70's, my first ML7 had no such adornment, and I relied on added arrangements using a toolmakers clamp or G clamp. Later, two Colchester lathes came along, each fitted with maker's stops (one micrometer, one five way) and the present Myford S7 sports the manufacturer's five way stop. It will be possible to design and make a stop, perhaps micro adjustable, or multiway for the Mini lathe, but for getting started quickly, the low cost of the Chinese item really makes it a no brainer. As **Photo 4.19** shows,

4.21 Parts after modification.

it is not perfect in that the clamp plate can move out of alignment, but that does not upset the clamping. If you have a drilling machine, then this undesirable feature can be easily rectified as described below. If the Mini lathe is your only workshop machine tool, then the rework can be accomplished using the optional vertical slide milling attachment, which will be examined later.

Brief digression (2)

To improve the carriage stop will take just a few minutes. After removing it from the lathe, tighten the clamp screw whilst

*keeping the two parts in line. Locate in a vice and drill a hole of 1/8in. diameter to a depth of 10mm as shown in **Photo 4.20.** Separate the parts and open up the hole in the plate by drilling through with a number 30 or 3.5mm drill (clearance for 1/8th). Cut off a short (say 12mm) length of 1/8th in. diameter silver steel, debur the ends, and Loctite in the hole. **Photo 4.21** shows the components after modification. Following reassembly, the pin will hold the plate in line, improving the appearance and giving more of a quality feel.*

Getting started - safety

Before proceeding to fire up the machine, a few words on safety may be in order. In the past some readers have criticised what they interpret as my cavalier approach to safety. This, I hasten to add, is something of a misconception. Now nearing the end of a career which has seen much time in the engineering industry and some in the motor trade, I can, at the time of writing, count a full complement of fingers, toes, eyes and ears. If I take risks, then they are likely to have been assessed. Certainly, I would not be so naively idiotic as to for instance place delicate digits below heavy items, which might be subject to the obviously foreseeable effect of that generally well understood phenomenon, i.e. gravity.

Although this is a small machine a few precautions should be taken, so no ties, long hair or loose clothing that could wrap around a rotating chuck or workpiece. With any machining operation, safety glasses or a face shield would be a good idea. This is particularly true when working on brass, as 1) the swarf comes off as fine needles at high speed, 2) if you do get one of these in your eye, then the people at A&E cannot remove it with a magnet and will probably spend some time poking about to retrieve the debris. Furthermore this is likely to be without a general anaesthetic. (Back in the 60's, Rolls-Royce used to show to all apprentices an eye safety film, which followed the progress of such an incident. Usually one or two fainted, but the point was well made) Brass swarf also has an annoying habit of becoming embedded in fingers, so a magnifying glass and tweezers may be useful. Brass splinters not removed have a habit of causing inflammation and pain. From some grades of steel, the swarf may be generated as long ribbons. Treat these as if they were razor blades, so do not grab or poke a finger into a loop and pull.

If you are using an extension cable, make sure it has an effective earth. With the growth in popularity of double insulated hand tools, I have seen orange cables, which have only line and neutral; these are not suitable for extension sockets.

A first exercise

The instruction manual recommends that before switching on the power, the speed should be set to zero, then power on then set forward, then increase the speed setting. Likewise the makers recommend that the speed be reduced to zero then set to off. This is probably a bit extreme, but avoids the possibility of trying to start heavy work at maximum speed, which might cause the overload to trip.

As a first turning exercise aimed at beginners, I am proposing the first of several components, which will form a headstock-dividing device. The principle is well proven, using a changewheel e.g.

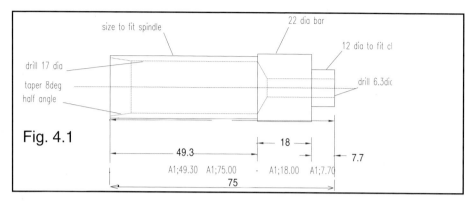

Fig. 4.1

size to fit spindle

22 dia bar

12 dia to fit cl

drill 17 dia

taper 8deg
half angle

drill 6.3dia

49.3

18

7.7

A1;49.30   A1;75.00   ·   A1;18.00   A1;7.70

75

50 or 60 tooth to give divisions for a variety of numbers. To make this, a length of 7/8in. or 22mm diameter mild steel bar is needed, ideally the free machining variety. The component drawing is given as **Fig. 4.1.**

Before starting, measure the bore of the spindle at the rear of the headstock, as we are aiming to achieve a rattle free easy sliding fit here. The subject machine measured some 20.4mm diameter i.e. a little over the nominal 20mm. The bar was in the 3 jaw, and using a right hand knife tool the first end was faced. If using a high speed steel tool, then a speed of around 400rpm would be a typical maximum. With carbide, you could run quite a good deal faster but we are not out to set production records. The variable speed facility allows you to try different speeds and see what sounds and feels best. The C3 does give the option of engaging power feed, but on small machines I prefer to do things manually. First it gives you some feel for what is happening, and secondly, where the same leadscrew is used for feed and for screwcutting, (as on the Myford Sevens) my personal preference (having a view to long term accuracy) is to keep it exclusively for the latter.

The machining sequence I adopted, was based on my usual practice with larger machines, and offers an object lesson for working with smaller ones. After facing to a length of 75mm, I turned the O D to down to 20.35mm for a length of 49.3mm then drilled out to 17mm for a depth of about the same dimension. The instruction leaflet notes "We recommend that for rough cutting, you do not exceed 0.010in. (0.25mm) as your depth of cut". I am not sure if some one is just playing safe here, but I certainly took cuts well in excess of this and the machine coped admirably. It was noticeable that if high gear was selected, that the rpm drop under load was more than in low gear. The drilling was done in stages, 10mm 13mm then 17mm. If you do not have a 17mm drill, then use a boring bar to cut this hole. The 17mm drill is probably pushing the capacity envelope, and while being a bit heavy handed, I did manage to get the overload to trip. After resetting, the operation continued, and by feeding more gently and by making sure the speed drop under load was only about 20 rpm, all went well.

The topslide was then set over 8

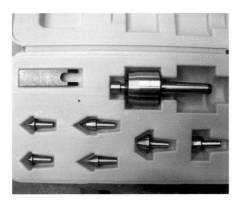

Above: 4.22 Live centre kit . Right: 4.23 Using the Live Centre Kit to support the workpiece.

degrees and a boring bar used to cut the conical bore feature. Now comes the object lesson. With my other machines, I would simply reverse the work and load into the chuck up to the shoulder. However here the chuck has only a 16mm bore so a much larger overhang resulted. This combined with the flexibility of the thin tubular wall meant that the work moved and the tool dug in almost straightaway when even a light cut was attempted, causing slight surface damage to the O.D. The remedy was to reposition the work, centre drill the end and add support with a tailstock centre. For this, the supplied centre proved less than ideal because its length would be insufficient to allow tool access to the end of the work. Fortunately, another of the accessories supplied by Arc is their Multi Purpose Live Centre Set, **(Photo 4.22)** which includes a No.2 Morse taper live centre body with seven interchangeable centre adapters. With this

in place **(Photo 4.23)** cutting the 12mm diameter became a doddle, using a changewheel to check for fit. The final operation here was to drill the hole through 1/4in diameter as clearance for M6.

If I had thought more about the sequence before getting stuck in, I might have adopted one of two alternative strategies. Either machine the 12mm diameter first, and avoid the problem, or fit the 4 jaw chuck and be able to accommodate the diameter within the body of the chuck.

Observations after initial experience

The limitations of the tailstock barrel and centre extension were touched on above. It may also be noted that if a Morse taper with tang extension is employed, then as occurs with most lathes, some reduction of effective tailstock barrel movement results. The saddle stop was modified as described above, and a second alteration is now in prospect. This is because the socket head of the Allen screw used to secure the clamp is nicely positioned to collect small particles of swarf, and this makes it less easy to engage the Allen key. Since preparing these notes, the Allen screw has been replaced with a short length of studding Loctited to the lower plate, and clamped with a nut. This will give a further advantage in that the thread in the plate becomes static and any wear over time will take place on the rod and nut, both of which are easily replaceable.

Another area in which swarf may lodge is the apron This is open on the side facing the leadscrew, which allows small bits of swarf to get in amongst the gear teeth, causing a roughness which can be felt when turning the carriage handwheel and adding a cover will be a straightforward modification but yet to be addressed.

One other storage aid may be worthy of mention. Rather than have the change wheels loose in the drawer, the gadget shown in **Photo 4.24** keeps them together

4.24 *"Quickie" storage for changewheels.*

and can be knocked up in less than five minutes. It is simply a short length of bar (say between 8 and 10mm diameter) set in a chipboard base.

Chapter 5

Gear Cover and Headstock Dividing Attachment

During the last chapter, I commented on a couple of shortcomings, namely the open backed apron, which allowed swarf to get in amongst the gear teeth, and the saddle stop for which an initial modification was described. It was also proposed to change the socket head clamp screw - (fine swarf got into the socket) - for a stud and nut, and this has now been done as may be seen from some of the Photos.

Apron cover

To stop swarf entering the gears, I have now added a cover made from a piece of polycarbonate sheet. Why this material, well because I had a bit left over from making racing car windows a few years ago. It's the plastic used for riot shields, so should also be suitable to withstand the slings and arrows of outrageous engineering malpractice. It's probably a bit of an overkill, and a suitable cover might be made of almost any thin sheet material-

metal, plywood, hardboard, plastic etc. In fact, while putting this one together, it did occur to me that Blue Peter aficionados might even use cardboard salvaged from a breakfast cereal packet, glued in place. Taking things in the other direction, if you check out some of the Mini Lathe web sites, at least one enthusiast has added a more substantial cover, and then used it to house bearings to give added support to the apron gears, perhaps even more of an overkill.

The first stage in this exercise is to remove the apron. After undoing the two Allen screws which secure the apron to the saddle, and those holding the right hand leadscrew bearing in place, the bearing is removed. Now, with the half nuts open, the apron may be slid along to the right and off the end of the leadscrew. The bearing was then bolted back in place so that the machine could be used, albeit with no apron assembly.

It is now possible to check whether

5.1. Straight edge indicated gears are proud of apron casing.

5.2. Facing small gear.

the thickness of the gears takes them proud of the housing surface. **Photo 5.1** shows a straight edge laid across. Using feeler gauges it was found that one gear was about 0.0020 in. proud, and the other about 0.0012 in.

The bearing surface of the smaller gear was then protected by wrapping a strip of thin aluminium around it prior to gripping in the 3-jaw chuck chuck. The saddle was then pushed towards the chuck, and the saddle stop set at a suitable position. Facing **(Photo 5.2)** was then

accomplished by holding the saddle against the stop with one hand while applying cross feed with the other. Axial increments were effected using the top slide.

As was mentioned previously, the 3-jaw chuck chuck is bored through 16mm so would not take the larger gear. The 4-jaw chuck (which is bored through 25mm) was therefore fitted. Whereas the 3-jaw attaches directly to the spindle, the 4-jaw chuck is attached via a backplate (which is drilled to accept either the 4-jaw chuck

5.3. Large gear held in 4-jaw chuck, teeth protected by card.

5.4. Blank roughly sawn to shape.

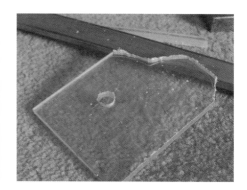

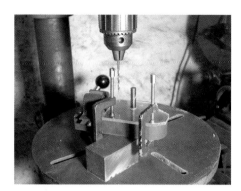

5.5. Drilling prior to tapping 5BA.

5.6. Aluminium bar used to keep tap vertical.

or larger 3-jaw chuck chuck). After bolting chuck to backplate, the three setcrews were withdrawn from the 3-jaw chuck, fitted to the backplate, and this in turn bolted to the spindle.

The gear was then gripped on its periphery, using a strip of cardboard **(Photo 5.3)** as protection for the teeth. As the cut would be a simple facing operation over the protruding boss, no attempt was made to accurately centre the work.

After facing off the few thou needed to give clearance, both gears were then assembled back in the housing. A quick recheck with the straight edge confirmed that a little clearance was now present.

Attention then turned to making the sheet cover, which was first cut to a rectangle of approximately 90mm by 70mm. Others may choose a different sequence of operations, but I chose the following.

The position of the gear spindle was measured as being 34mm in from the edge of the half nuts and 25mm down from the top surface of the housing. Two reasonably accurate edges on the sheet were chosen and an 8mm hole drilled at this position. The sheet could then be placed

over the back of the apron and clamped in place. A scriber was run around the periphery of the apron, and the cover cut roughly to shape **(Photo 5.4).** Here I chose to use the bandsaw, but it would not take long with a good old-fashioned hacksaw or coping saw. It was then once more clamped in position on the apron.

Three holes were then drilled 2.65mm dia. and here the transparent plastic gives an advantage **(Photo 5.5)** in that you can see what part of the apron you are drilling into. The depth of drilling was about 12mm into the metal. After dismantling, the holes in the plastic were opened up to 3.3mm while those in the apron were tapped 5BA. (I have used BA because I have some of these screws, but for those with metric kit, M2.5 or M3 would be quite suitable.

For those with limited experience of tapping in the smaller sizes, it may be worth noting that the principal causes of tap breakage are misalignment, bluntness and chip compaction. I don't own a George Thomas Universal Pillar Tool, so rely on a very rudimentary piece of equipment to keep small taps perpendicular to

5.7. Boring clearance hole using 4-jaw chuck.

5.8. Apron assembly with cover fitted.

the job. It is nothing more than a short length of 5/8in. square aluminium, drilled through with several holes, which relate to different tap sizes. It can be seen in **Photo 5.6**. The aluminium is held firmly against the work, keeping the tap in correct alignment. Concerning the latter two breakage causes, if a tap starts to feel more resistant, try another and if necessary scrap one that has lost its edge unless you are confident about sharpening. Chip compaction can occur when a hand tap is driven forwards without regular reversal to break the chips. If the chips are allowed to fill the flutes and jam, then breakage is likely to result.

Once the cover was located and secured by the three screws, the outside edges could be filed to shape close to the outside of the apron. It was then necessary to open up the 8mm hole to a little over 17mm to clear the gear and shaft. This was done by mounting the work in the 4-jaw chuck chuck, **(Photo 5.7)**, centring up more carefully this time, before drilling out to 13mm prior to boring to 17.5mm. Note

that due to the shape of the work, pressure was applied mainly by the two opposed jaws in contact with the parallel sides. The other two were really just nipped up, as one was making corner contact, risking indenting the job if excessively tightened. An alternative method here would have utilised the faceplate, but as it was found that the job could be mounted in the chuck, which was already in place, it was more convenient to proceed in this way.

At this stage the various parts were cleaned, the edges of the gear teeth treated to a rub with a wire brush, then reassembled with fresh grease **(Photo 5.8).**

The leadscrew bearing was once again removed and the apron refitted again bearing in mind the comments made previously about progressively nipping up, minimising leadscrew endfloat and achieving best alignment.

4-jaw chuck - notes on centring for beginners

This exercise had seen the first applications of the 4-jaw chuck, the first of

5.9. Centring using DTI on magnetic base from bed.

5.10. DTI clamped to tool post.

which needed no particular attention to centring, whereas the second did. A few comments on this may benefit beginners. Ideally the process is conducted using a DTI or clock gauge which may be mounted on a magnetic base, **(Photo 5.9)** or on a bar mounted in the toolpost **(Photo 5.10).** However if one of these has not yet found its way into the armoury, work can still be accurately centred using just the lathe.

With the job located in the chuck, the jaws being only lightly tightened, clamp a length of metal bar in the toolpost so that using the cross slide, it can be moved in to contact the work. (The bar may be anything convenient even a tool mounted back to front **(Photo 5.11).** A softer material will be less likely to mark the job.) Then back off the cross slide so that the chuck can be rotated by hand. Looking down as the work is rotated it will be possible to make initial corrections by eye, slackening one jaw a little, then gently tightening the one opposite.

To improve on this, set one pair of jaws horizontal and gently move the cross slide in to make contact. Note the dial reading. Back off, rotate 180 degrees and repeat. The difference in the readings is twice the eccentricity of the job, so the aim is to move this pair of jaws by half the difference, and reduce the error to zero. It will probably take several attempts, but you should get there.

The process is then repeated for the second pair of jaws. Once a constant

5.11. Backing a tool in to touch.

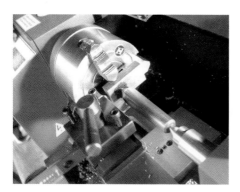

5.12. Second MT centre locates in centre pop.

5.13. Dividing attachment fitted to Mini-Lathe.

reading has been obtained at all 4-jaws then they may each be fully tightened in preparation for work. The final tightening should be done a little at a time, rechecking the readings at each stage.

It was noted that until the final stage, the jaws were not tightened hard. This is because the shifting of one pair of jaws forces the work to slide across the ends of the second pair. If tight this will cause surface damage to the work and may make accurate centring more difficult.

To centre an item such as the hole in the part made cover, it can be helpful to position a Morse taper centre between the tailstock and the work. This technique may also be used on work such as that shown in **Photo 5.12** where the feature may be no more than a centre pop. When working against a taper, it is important to maintain a constant carriage position, perhaps against the saddle stop.

One of the accessories supplied for the Mini-Lathe is the set of Digital Read Out (DRO) handwheels for the cross slide and top slide. Whilst undertaking the centring exercise, it did occur to me that with the

DRO fitted to the cross slide, centring up would be made that bit more convenient, effectively doing the job of a clock gauge.

Returning to the dividing attachment. In the previous chapter, a turning exercise was proposed which would form the first component (the expanding arbor) of a headstock dividing attachment. The finished device is shown in **Photo 5.13**, and allows work held in the chuck to be rotated by accurate angles or indexed using a change gear to give appropriate numbers of divisions. Using such a gadget, it becomes possible to cut divisions on items such as micrometer handwheels, or to undertake indexing work using a toolpost grinder or drill.

Constructing the dividing attachment will also provide the opportunity to make a further convenience modification to the lathe. As standard the cover is held in place by two long Allen screws, and so to remove the cover, you need to find the key. The change substitutes two 88mm lengths of M5 studding and a pair of knurled thumbnuts, these parts being required, in any case, for the attachment.

5.14. Centre drilling the body.

Plunger Body

While the 4-jaw chuck was in place, the opportunity was taken to make the plunger body **(Fig 5.1)**. This was a piece of 7/8 by 1/2in. flat bar sawn to a length of 36mm. This was then mounted in the chuck, and here, the work was positioned so that identical centring readings were obtained against three faces. This then gave the correct offset. The end was first faced, followed by centre drill **(Photo 5.14)** and 15/64in. drill to a depth of 25mm. After this the hole was continued through using a

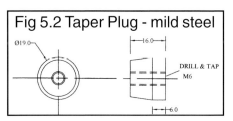

Fig 5.2 Taper Plug - mild steel

4mm drill, and a 1/4in. reamer used to open up the main bore. The work was then reversed in the chuck and face back to 35mm length. (Note that I chose 1/4in. as I had a reamer of this size. If you have a 6mm then by all means change the sizes. If you do not yet have a reamer, drill 15/64in. and then follow with the 1/4in. drill. This will not give the smoothness or accuracy of a reamed finish, but will be adequate. In any case, the plunger will be made to fit the bore)

Taper plug

With lathe work on the body complete, the 3-jaw chuck chuck was refitted, and the next component, the taper plug, considered. For this a short length of 19mm dia. steel bar is needed. Work simply entails facing to about 16mm length, then, with about 10mm

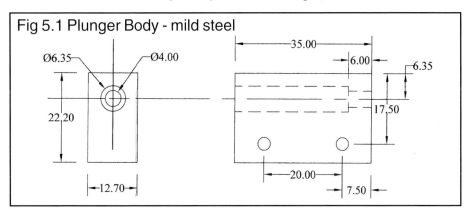

Fig 5.1 Plunger Body - mild steel

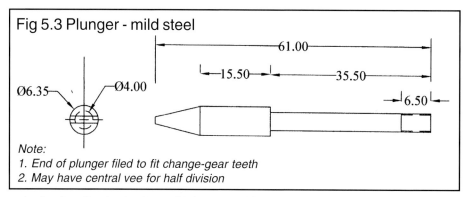

Fig 5.3 Plunger - mild steel

Ø6.35

Ø4.00

61.00

15.50

35.50

6.50

Note:
1. End of plunger filed to fit change-gear teeth
2. May have central vee for half division

protruding from the chuck, a taper of 8 degree half angle is turned so that it will enter the conical bore in the arbor. It is then drilled and tapped M6 as shown in **Fig 5.2**. The spindle insert or arbor, previously described, was then given four axial slots cut with a hacksaw. A length of M6 screwed rod, two nuts, and a 1/4 - 3/4in. washer then completed this subassembly which, with a typical change wheel fitted, is shown with the other components in **Photo 5.15**. From this Photo it can be seen that the 125mm of studding that I used is a little on the long side so 105mm would be more appropriate.

Plunger and spring

The spring details are as follows O D 5.5mm, wire dia. 0.6mm, free length 32mm, compressed (coil bound) length 12mm. This was a spring purchased as part of a bargain bulk pack at a woodworking exhibition, and the size looked suitable. The size of spring has to work with the diameters of plunger and body, so if you have a spring which is a little different, then by all means adjust the design to suit. Details of the plunger are given in **Fig 5.3**, and I chose to make it from a length of 3/8in. dia. free cutting mild

5.15. Component parts of attachment.

5.16. Cutting the thread on the plunger.

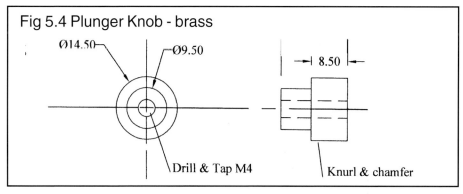

Fig 5.4 Plunger Knob - brass

Ø14.50

Ø9.50

8.50

Drill & Tap M4

Knurl & chamfer

steel rod. My method was to start with just a short length say 10 or 12mm protruding from the chuck. This was faced, centred then turned down to 3.9mm for a length of about 8mm. (Taking it a little below 4mm would give the die an easier time cutting the thread and would ensure clearance for the tool in the proximity of the tailstock.) The bar was then drawn out of the chuck sufficiently to turn the full length, and the tailstock brought up for support. The 4mm and 1/4in. diameters were then turned, then the thread added using a die. As can be seen in **Photo 5.16**, the die was held in a hand diestock, kept square to the job with a female tailstock centre, whilst the chuck was rotated by hand. The job was then removed from the lathe, cut slightly over length using a hacksaw then returned to the chuck for facing to length.

A brief digression on parting-off
Some will no doubt disagree here, and advocate using a part off tool. Back in the seventies, my efforts to use a part off tool mounted in the front toolpost on my Myford ML7 were sometimes successful, but also

sometimes resulted in dig in and tool breakage. Later on, larger machines came equipped with rear toolposts and parting off with these was a revelation. The reason has been discussed at various times in these pages and is due to the deflection path of the tool tip under cutting loads: a rear tool moves upwards and outwards reducing the cut, while its front mounted counterpart moves downwards and inwards, digging in.

As a consequence I just do not attempt parting off with a front tool and either remove the work to the bench, or cut a shallow groove with a vee tool and use this to guide the saw

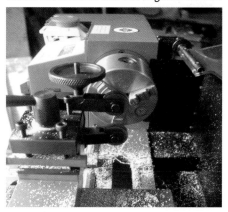

5.17. Arc knurling tool fitted to lathe.

5.18. Tap wrench steadied from tailstock rotated by hand.

Plunger Knob

This is a simple turned item, which I chose to make from brass. It could equally be from steel or aluminium, but brass was available and is aesthetically pleasing. The details are given in **Fig 5.4** but it should be noted that none of the dimensions are critical, as long as it screws on to the end of the plunger and gives something to grip to pull against the spring.

It does however offer an opportunity to try out the knurling tool **(Photo 5.17)** supplied by Arc. On this machine it might be thought a little oversize, as careful positioning is needed to avoid blanking a clamp screw by the pressure handwheel. Nevertheless a knurled finish was quickly obtained.

To tap the M4 thread, the tap was held in a small hand Tee tap wrench steadied from the tailstock **(Photo 5.18),** the tap being rotated by hand.

A brief digression on knurling

Knurling is applied here to give "non slip" surface to aid grip. The process moves the metal creating ridges and furrows, by forcing patterned rollers into the surface. Simple knurling tools may have one or two knurls which rely on pressure being applied directly from the toolpost. This is fine for heavy-duty industrial machines, but at the hobby size, straddle, (or pinch or clamp) types are more suitable as they contain the heavy forces within the tool. Nevertheless, there is still significant sideways pressure and so a long component should be supported.

Having turned the diameter to be treated, the tool is brought into position and adjusted to match the diameter. It is then withdrawn and the handwheel tightened down perhaps a half turn. If

whilst the work is held in the machine.

The final operations on the plunger were carried out by careful filing and sawing. The aim is for the end to fit neatly to the change gear teeth, removing equal amounts from each side. The plunger may be engaged in two positions by rotating through 90 degrees. Either the "screwdriver" style end lodges between two teeth, or in the alternative position, it sits between three teeth, one of which projects into a shaped slot in the end of the plunger. The advantage of this arrangement is that it allows a doubling up of the available divisions. Thus a fifty-tooth changewheel may be used to produce 100 divisions for a hand wheel scale. Again, for this to work accurately, the slot must be central to the plunger.

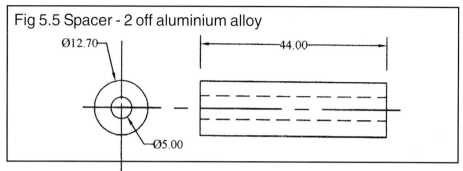

Fig 5.5 Spacer - 2 off aluminium alloy

Ø12.70

44.00

Ø5.00

space permits, the tool is then positioned lengthways so that about half the width of the rolls will engage reducing the initial load, then with spindle speed at say a quarter of that used for turning, moved inwards using the cross slide. Infeed is stopped at the point when it reaches the centre. This can be felt as a change in load at the finger tips while feeding. The carriage is then moved axially to widen the knurled area as needed.

Knurling can be a bit hit and miss as regards achieving the intended pattern; sometimes a double pattern results as may be seen in the case of this brass part. If you are doing a production run, then a few trials will usually lead to a pressure setting which

gives a consistent and correct appearance. With a one off it is not always the case. Note that the aluminium thumb nuts made later were given a bit more pressure and came out with excellent knurling.

Spacers

Two spacers are needed, the details being shown in **Fig 5.5**. Producing these is a straightforward matter of cutting slightly over length, then facing to length, followed by centring and drilling. As the length is large compared to the drill diameter, it is advisable to drill about halfway from each end.

Thumb nuts

As mentioned above, these nuts **(Fig 5.6)**

5.19. This time tapping under power.

5.20. Chamfering with vee tool.

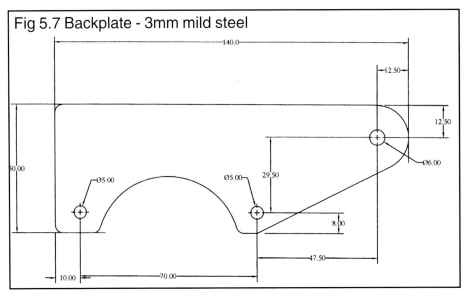

Fig 5.7 Backplate - 3mm mild steel

140.0
12.50
12.50
Ø6.00
50.00
Ø5.00
Ø5.00
29.50
8.00
47.50
10.00
70.00

may be used in conjunction with two 88mm lengths of M5 screwed rod to replace the gear cover fixings. The procedure for manufacture of the nuts is very similar to that adopted for the plunger knob above, except that part of the bore is drilled away to reduce the length of thread and speed up fitting the nuts. Here the low

speed capability of the machine was explored for the tapping operation. A spiral flute M5 machine tap was gripped in the tailstock chuck **(Photo 5.19)** and the lathe run slowly forwards. Flicking to reverse and raising the speed a little gave a quicker

5.21. Backplate marked out with felt tipped pen.

Fig 5.5 Thumbnut - aluminium alloy 2 off

Ø12.70
Ø8.00
Knurl & Chamfer
23.50
Drill 6 x 7 deep
Drill & Tap M6
8.00

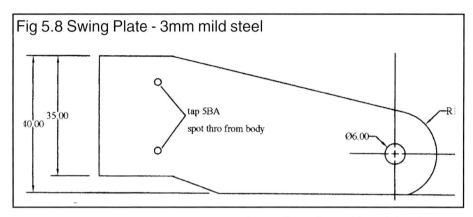

Fig 5.8 Swing Plate - 3mm mild steel

exit. Note that machine taps (spiral point and spiral flute) are designed to be driven through, or to the required depth, in one pass. Once again, the knurling tool was employed, this time with extra pressure giving a first class result first time. A vee tool was then set up **(Photo 5.20)** to chamfer the edges of the knurled diameter.

Mounting plates

The two remaining parts are the main backplate and a moveable swing plate. The

latter allows the position of the plunger to be moved radially in order to accommodate different sizes of changewheel.

The backplate is shown in **Fig 5.7** and the swingplate in **Fig 5.8**, both being made from 3mm steel plate. The material I used was actually black steel strip, not very pretty, but quite functional. For the back plate, a length was cut, then the three 6mm holes marked out and drilled. The plate was then jury rigged on the machine to scientifically determine the clearance profile. In other

5.22. Plates and body part made.

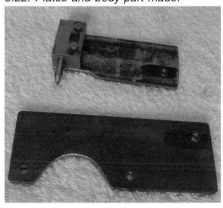

5.23. Gear cover retained by thumb nuts.

words marked out **(Photo 5.21)** with a felt tipped pen, so that the offending material could be cleared with saw, file etc. A 25mm diameter button was bolted to the pivot hole to give a guide to material removal at that end.

Work on the swing plate followed a similar pattern, and following trial assembly, the plunger body was clamped in place so that the two 5BA hole positions could be spotted through, then drilled and tapped.

The 5BA screws were then cut and filed to give a flush rear face to the swing plate. **Photo 5.22** shows the plates with body assembly at an interim stage before removal of more surplus material.

Finishing touches

Rust is a constant problem in my workshop, so I elected to paint the two plates and oil black some of the other steel parts. Paint is not an ideal solution as it will be liable to chipping and rubbing with movement, but due to their size, it was felt that attempting oil blacking on these might constitute a fire risk. The finished attachment was shown earlier in **Photo 5.13** and finally, **Photo 5.23** shows the gear cover now retained by the two aluminium thumb nuts.

Chapter 6

Modifications for Milling

In the previous chapter, I commented briefly on parting off, and noted that I just do not attempt this with a conventional front mounted tool. It may be possible to add a rear toolpost to the Mini Lathe, or consider another approach, but that is an exercise for another day. For now I will continue to either saw off in the machine or remove the work to bench vice or bandsaw. Sawing work off in the chuck carries the risk of

damaging the bed with the saw blade, so a quick exercise is to make a guard/cover which can be put in place to ensure that the saw does not contact the bed.

Various arrangements may be considered. I have chosen a simple assembly of three pieces of wood, cut, sanded and glued. Another eminently suitable alternative might be a piece of sheet metal, folded into a shallow "U". The machine bed measures about 83mm across, so aim to have a millimetre or so clearance. On width, I opted for about 75mm. and the finished gadget is shown in **Photo 6.1.**

Milling in the Lathe

For many purchasers, the C3 may represent the first significant foray into the world of the home metalworking workshop. It is therefore likely that while owners may also possess a small vertical bench drill,

6.1.Bed protector made from MDF.

milling facilities are not yet to hand. It is not so many years ago that small mills were something of a rarity and pretty expensive; it was therefore commonplace to undertake small scale milling work in the lathe.

One of the accessories offered by Arc for use with the C3 is a Vertical Slide, which can be fitted in place of the tool post. The

6.2. Vertical slide for the C3 lathe supplied by Arc Euro Trade.

slide, **(Photo 6.2)** carries clamping screws which may be used for securing work which can then be milled in the lathe. It might also be used as a variable height toolpost for turning work and in this guise could allow larger than normal turning tools to be employed. Before introducing work with this unit, I believe it will be useful to consider, in the first instance, a modification to the lathe, and in the second the construction of a simple accessory to use with the vertical slide. The modification will improve the accuracy and convenience when undertaking such work, and consists of the addition of a graduated handwheel for the leadscrew. With one of these fitted, the halfnuts may be closed (change gears being disengaged) and the saddle moved along the bed with a high degree of precision. Arc supply chrome handwheels which may be used to upgrade the black plastic standard items, so the exercise has been executed using one of these for the leadscrew and then a further two to replace the plastic wheels on the tailstock and the apron. Converting fully to these chromed cast wheels gives a marked increase in the feel

6.3. Facing the hex material.

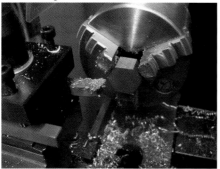

6.4. Tapping a nut under power.

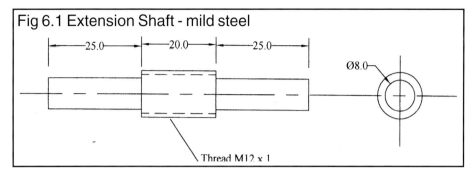

Fig 6.1 Extension Shaft - mild steel

25.0   20.0   25.0

Ø8.0

Thread M12 x 1

of quality when working with the machine.

Modification

In standard form, the right hand end of the leadscrew terminates flush with the associated bearing, so to accommodate the handwheel, an extension is required, the details being given in **Fig 6.1**. It is located in a holed drilled 8mm diameter, slightly more than 25mm deep, and is retained by Loctite. Adding the extension also presents the opportunity to provide a more sophisticated form of leadscrew end float adjustment. This is achieved by having two nuts running on an M12 x 1 thread.

Nuts

When screwcutting, it makes sense to have a nut or tapped part to use as a thread gauge. Having chosen M12 x 1 to give a

fine degree of adjustment, the first part of the process is to make the nuts. Start by sawing off a couple of slices of 19mm AF hex bar one about 9mm thick, the other about 13mm. Each is faced in the 3-jaw chuck **(Photo 6.3)**, then drilled through 11mm, and tapped. As can be seen from **Photo 6.4**, the tap was held in a tailstock chuck, and the machine run slowly in low gear, while the tailstock was pushed gently towards the work. The variable speed and reverse facility then made it easy to run back at higher speed saving a little time. **Figs 6.2a** and **6.2b** give the details of these parts

Extension shaft

As I had pushed ahead with the project, in advance of receiving the hand wheel, one or two slight differences may be discerned between the drawing and the photo.

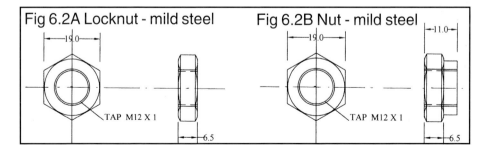

Fig 6.2A Locknut - mild steel

19.0

TAP M12 X 1

6.5

Fig 6.2B Nut - mild steel

19.0

11.0

TAP M12 X 1

6.5

6.5. Turning the first section of the extension shaft.

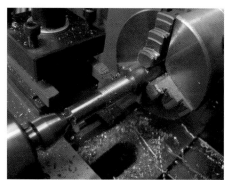

6.6. Screwcutting the shaft.

Specifically, handwheels are supplied with a bore of 8mm diameter and it makes sense to work to this. The length varies a little between wheels, one should be selected, and the shaft made to suit. The drawing shows 25mm at each end, and this should suffice.

A length of 12mm diameter free cutting mild steel bar is faced to a length of 70mm and centred at each end. With about 30mm protruding from the chuck, the first 8mm section is turned to 0.0010 in. or so undersize **(Photo 6.5)**.

The second 8mm diameter is handled in a similar way, and centred. The work is then chucked leaving perhaps 10mm clearance between the chuck and the 12mm section. This clearance will ease the screwcutting operation. (It may though be seen from **Photo 6.6**, that I handled the operations in a different order and so cut a relief groove for the threading tool to run into. It can also be seen that 10mm diameter had been adopted in advance of examining the chrome handwheels) Here, added support for the work is given by the tailstock, again using the multi centre kit. Setting up the change wheel train is straightforward, the details

as per the table given with the machine.

There are two schools of thought on screwcutting. The first believes that the topslide should be swung round to half the thread angle so that the tool is fed in parallel to one flank of the thread, and cuts only on one edge. As this would reduce the cutting load, it would be particularly applicable to lightweight machines such as the C3. When using this technique, it is important to remember that the overall amount of infeed will be increased due to the angle. For a metric thread of 1mm pitch, the depth of thread is 0.613mm, so feeding in at 30 degrees would increase this figure by a factor of 1/Cos30 degrees to 0.708mm.

The second line of thinking is probably held predominantly by those with a background in industrial machining. Here the top slide is left in its normal position, (presumably to save time), and feed movements made mainly radially with the cross slide, but with axial changes using the top slide. Because, for some of the time, the tool may be cutting on both edges, the loads on the machine are correspondingly higher. It may have been slightly unfair to choose this method on

Left: 6.7. An extended centre drill gets to places others cannot reach. Above: 6.8. Handwheel with graduated collar and friction rivet.

such a relatively small machine, but it passed with flying colours.

Here the variable speed and forward/reverse control proved a great advantage, in that the cut could be taken slowly forward, then stopped as the tool moved into fresh air. The cross slide was then backed out to bring the tool clear of the job before switching to reverse and dialling up a higher speed to return. Note that after closing the half nuts to start the thread cutting process, they remain closed until completion. I took an initial series of cuts, feeding in 0.1mm each time and intermittently moving the topslide across by a similar amount. (It is possible to work with a combined feed of 0.1mm on the cross slide and 0.05mm - topslide which will give nearly the same effect as setting the topslide over to 30 degrees)

Once the radial infeed passed 0.5mm,

the increment was reduced to 0.05mm and the size checked with a nut after each cut. This process was continued until it became possible to run the nut smoothly along the length of the thread. If you have a suitable thread chaser/file, then this can be used in combination with the screwcutting process to give a bit of rounding to the thread crests.

Leadscrew Handwheel

The 80mm dia. spoked chrome handwheels supplied by Arc (stock number 084-14-00080) are ideal for this application) and matching handles are also available. As noted above, these wheels may also be used as an "upgrade" for both the tailstock and apron to replace the standard plastic items. As supplied these wheels feature a plain diameter of roughly 29mm by 16mm in length and this makes an ideal location for a graduated indexable micrometer dial collar. Three of these wheels were obtained together with M6 handles. This approach would allow a micrometer collar to be added to the tailstock wheel, and an "approximately" graduated wheel to the apron.

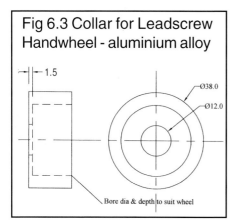

Fig 6.3 Collar for Leadscrew Handwheel - aluminium alloy

1.5

⌀38.0

⌀12.0

Bore dia & depth to suit wheel

6.9. Boring the collar.

For this first wheel I chose to arrange a position for the retaining grub screw located axially between this plain diameter and the wheel rim. To do this required a bit of careful positioning and the use of an extended centre drill, as shown in **Photo 6.7**. (A standard centre drill Loctited into an extension rod) It occurred to me later that the retaining screw might actually be positioned along the plain diameter, provided an access hole is drilled in the collar, to allow access for an Allen key to the clamping screw.

An indexable collar needs a bit of friction to ensure that it retains its setting but can still be moved without undue force. The first experiment used heavy grease between collar and wheel, and this simple approach may be suitable depending on the consistency of your chosen grease. The solution actually adopted employs a blind hole drilled radially, containing a small spring which pushes a shortened rivet outwards to contact the inner diameter of the collar. The parts are shown in **Photo 6.8**. In the case of the leadscrew wheel, all of the components in contact rotate together, so the need for friction is not so

great. Other methods of introducing the friction effect may include turning a groove in the wheel to accommodate either an O ring or short bent spring as on the existing cross slide and topslide dials.

Graduated collar

Before proceeding to make the collar, **(Fig 6.3)** first measure carefully the plain diameter of the new wheel? The three wheels used here showed a diameter variation of roughly a millimetre, and about the same on length, so collars are made to match each wheel. The aim is to have the collar slide easily over the wheel, and be a few thou less in thickness than the length of the shoulder.

A slice of 38mm diameter aluminium was faced both ends, a millimetre or so over length, then drilled through 12mm. Using the wheel as a gauge, the interior was then bored out **(Photo 6.9)** to give an easy shake free fit. It was then measured for length, and the amount to be machined off checked by reference to the hand wheel.

6.10. Changewheel has been marked to indicate teeth to be used.

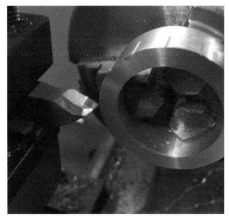

6.11. A vee tool has been mounted on its side to cut the divisions.

The work was then chucked with sufficient material protruding, and squared up by pushing gently into the chuck with the tool.

For those not familiar with the method, first lightly grip the work in the chuck, and set the saddle stop so that the tool is a few thou clear of the job. Then with number one jaw horizontal and towards you, move the saddle up to the stop and wind in the topslide to contact the work then another 0.005in. gently pushing the work into the chuck. Back off, rotate the spindle to bring No2 jaw into position and again bring the saddle towards the chuck. Repeat for jaw 3, (and 4 if using a 4-jaw chuck chuck). If at any of the stages, the tool did not contact the work, then advance the topslide a further 0.005in. and repeat the process. The work was then faced back to the required length.

To apply the graduations, the collar was held by its internal diameter in the 3-jaw chuck and the headstock indexing device, featured in a previous article, was fitted, utilising the 60 tooth change wheel. The pitch of the leadscrew (on the metric machine) is 1.5mm, so I opted to apply fifteen divisions with longer markings at 0, 5, 10. As a preliminary measure, white Tippex marking fluid was used to identify those teeth on the change wheel, which would be, used **(Photo 6.10).**

To cut the division marks, a vee tool was set in the tool post, but at 90 degrees to its normal position **(Photo 6.11).** The saddle stop was set so that the tool travel would be checked partway along the work, fine adjustment then being made by the topslide.

The three major long marks were

6.12. Three pieces of MDF serve as a punch guide.

6.13. Punch guide and work holder are clamped to a mill table.

6.14. Collet chuck used to grip the leadscrew.

tackled first. The spindle was rotated and latched into the first of the Tippexed major division teeth. The tool was moved in to contact the work, the saddle moved clear, the tool moved in five thou, then the saddle moved up to the stop to make the first cut. It was then moved clear, and the tool advanced in a further 0.005in. for a second bite, deepening the graduation. After the two other major divisions had been similarly completed, the topslide was wound back a few millimetres to give shorter lines for the other positions.

The final operation on this part was to add the stamped numerals. In the past I have applied number punches free hand with variable results. While there have been designs published for robust metal jigs, it is an operation which has not arisen sufficiently frequently for me to consider making such an accessory worth while. I therefore sought an easy method of aligning punch and work to give a reasonably tidy result. My number punches measure close to 0.250in, square in cross section, so three pieces of MDF glued together sufficed to make a punch guide **(Photo 6.12),** while the workpiece

6.15. Detail view of an ER32 collet and closing ring.

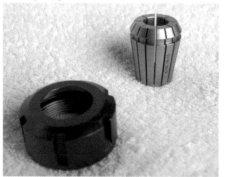

6.16. Pressure applied to the extension shaft by using the tailstock.

6.17. Leadscrew handwheel assembly fitted.

6.18. Brass disc for tailstock wheel.

was successfully located in a semicircular recess sawn in a piece of chipboard. These two items were clamped down **(Photo 6.13)** to the table on a large mill, but the same system might equally be held down on a convenient bench. Just aim to have the punch axis aligned with the centre of the work. One minor point worth noting is that the number one has less line length than the others and hence needs less "oomph" with the hammer.

Leadscrew modification

First remove the leadscrew as described in chapter 2, then all that is required is to drill the right hand end 8mm diameter by 25mm deep, so that the extension shaft may be inserted and retained with Loctite. To avoid the possibility of damage to the surface of the screw, I opted to grip the work using the ER32 collet chuck **(Photo 6.14)**. Again, this is an accessory available from Arc. A detail view of the particular collet and closing ring is given in **Photo 6.15**. If you choose to use a conventional chuck, then protect the work by placing thin aluminium or copper between it and the jaws. Once the drilling

work is completed, the extension shaft may be fitted. It was found that the Loctite trapped air in the cavity, which pushed the extension out. This was overcome by placing the components in the lathe **(Photo 6.16)** and applying pressure with the tailstock.

Assembly

The leadscrew was refitted to the machine then the two locknuts added. These were then adjusted to give free rotation with minimal end float. The handwheel and collar were then added. A bracket was then made from 20 swg sheet steel on which the static fiducial line was marked by gently applying a junior hacksaw. As can be seen in **Photo 6.17**, the cut lines have been filled (black on the aluminium, white on black painted steel). The paint used was the acrylic supplied in tubes for artists, smeared round with a finger, working into the grooves, then rubbed off after allowing to partially dry.

Tailstock and apron handwheels

The exercise here was then substantially

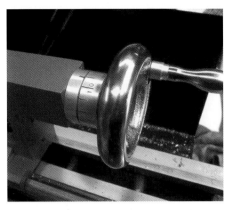

6.19. Tailstock wheel assembly with the new static collar fitted.

6.20. Handwheel mounted on faceplate.

similar to that for the leadscrew, except for the following design points.

• A 22g brass disc was made, seen near completed placed in position in **Photo 6.18**. It is clamped between the handwheel and the shoulder on the screw and retains the collar on the handwheel. It rotates with it, preventing the collar from contacting the static part of the assembly. Such contact might upset the setting.

• The divisions are as for the leadscrew, but the numerals progress in the opposite direction.

• A second collar was made mainly for appearance which fits over the black static thrust block, and is Loctited in place. A single fiducial line was marked again using the junior hacksaw, although, with the benefit of hindsight, this would be better done in the same way as the wheel collars.

This arrangement shown in **Photo 6.19** would now allow holes to be drilled to depth using the 0.1mm divisions, or perhaps judged by eye to even greater accuracy.

The tailstock wheel needs to be clamped up by its retaining screw, so its thickness was reduced to that of the original plastic, less the thickness of the brass disc. This was done in two operations. First the wheel was gripped in the 3-jaw chuck and the rear counterbored about three millimetres, then it was located on the faceplate **(Photo 6.20)**, to allow material to be removed at the opposite

6.21. Apron handwheel fitted with graduated collar.

6.22. Relative position of spindle and vertical slide at one extreme of travel.

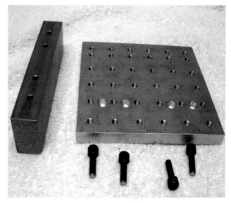

6.23. Two components form the sub table.

end. In this case the exercise to drill and tap the position for the grubscrew was exactly as before.

In the case of the apron, it was found that one turn of the wheel moved the saddle by approximately 19.2mm. It was felt that for rough turning to length, this might be approximated to 20mm. A collar was thus made carrying twenty minor divisions and numerals corresponding to majors at 0, 5, 10, and 15. This collar was retained with Loctite, and may be seen in **Photo 6.21**.

In an earlier article, it was noted that, on the apron wheel, the grubscrew engages in a drilled recess. It is therefore worth ensuring that the position is duplicated on the replacement wheel to ensure that the screw engages in the same way.

And now to milling

The vertical slide attachment was shown earlier off the machine in **Photo 6.2** and may be seen mounted in the 90degree position in **Photo 6.22**. As supplied it gives a good robust mounting allowing some 90mm of vertical movement. However it attaches in place of the toolpost and this

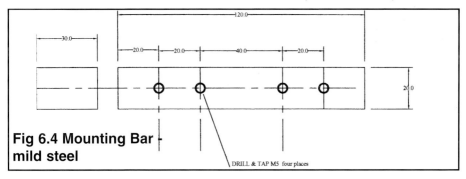

Fig 6.4 Mounting Bar mild steel

DRILL & TAP M5 four places

6.24. One piece of flat bar has been drilled to create five small clamps.

6.25. Clamps have been cut off, tidied up, and fitted with screws.

position compromises the convenience in use. The cross slide travel is some 70mm and thus milling work may be accomplished over a notional table area of 70 x 90mm, but as can be seen in **Photo 6.22**, when the cross slide is run inwards (limited by contact with the rear splashback), the centreline of the spindle is only partway across the clamping section. As an immediate and simple solution to this, I propose a form of sub table, which may be clamped in the "Vice", extending across to provide a useable miniature milling table. Added accessories for use with the table, are a number of small clamps, and a short length of bright mild steel angle used as a miniature angle

plate. Other clamping arrangements may be made to suit the requirements of specific jobs.

Sub table

This is made from two components, shown in **Photo 6.23** and **Figs 6.4** and **6.5**. These are assembled with M5 x 20 Allen screws. The table surface was cut from a piece of 3/8in. aluminium plate and finished to a rectangle of some 120mm by 110mm. As can be seen from the photo, the surface features a grid formation of rows of M5 tapped holes into which the clamps may be fastened. If you decide to construct something similar, you may of course choose a different pattern, or even leave the surface blank and simply add holes as necessary to suit the requirements of particular jobs.

The table stub (by which it is clamped into the vertical slide) is a piece of 30mm by 20mm BMS cut to 120mm in length. Note that this size may be varied to suit material to hand. For future convenience in aligning work horizontally or vertically on the table, it is worth making sure that

6.26. Two clamps used to hold a length of aluminium to the table.

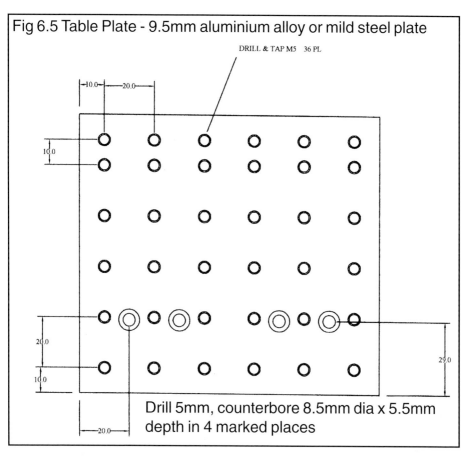

Fig 6.5 Table Plate - 9.5mm aluminium alloy or mild steel plate

DRILL & TAP M5   36 PL

Drill 5mm, counterbore 8.5mm dia x 5.5mm depth in 4 marked places

on assembly, the clamping stub is parallel with the top/bottom edges.

Clamps

The material used here was an off cut of 25mm by 6mm black steel flat bar. This allowed the holes to be marked out and drilled/tapped, **(Photo 6.24)** then the clamps to be cut off crosswise. Feel free

6.27. Milling sub table.

to work with other raw material that may be to hand. A strip of say 10mm x 6mm or even 8mm x 5mm would work equally well except that the individual pieces would be cut off lengthways. For convenience in manufacture, it is often easier to hold a larger part then a smaller, and hence my choice to drill and tap the holes before cutting off the individual pieces. The intermediate spots which can be seen in the Photo were used to guide the position for sawing.

Photo 6.25 shows a selection of the clamps with the small angle plate made from bright steel angle.

In use

Photo 6.26 shows the sub table fitted to the vertical slide, with a length of aluminium secured to the table by a couple of clamps. It is now possible to utilise the full travel of the cross slide along with that of the vertical slide, to perform light drilling operations, such as spotting the positions of holes. Due to the interrupted cutting action of a milling cutter, milling places great demands on a machine in terms of rigidity, if excessive vibration is to be avoided. The next chapter will consider methods of improving the rigidity to an extent that will permit effective milling work, and will also return to the topic of parting off.

Chapter 7

Improving Rigidity & Making a Part-Off Tool

The last chapter closed with the comment that added measures would be provided to enhance the rigidity for milling. Most turning involves continuous cutting and therefore a fairly consistent load on the tool. Thus under most circumstances, vibration due to the cutting action is not a major problem. Milling however is a rather different kettle of fish. A typical end mill with four edges, or slot drill with two, will take a corresponding number of bites during each revolution, and each bite will cause a sharp rise and fall in cutting load, which will tend to cause vibration. Changes to mitigate these effects are proposed in three areas: saddle clamps located at front left and rear right of the saddle, and clamp screws to lock or tighten the cross slide.

Saddle Clamps

Photo 7.1 shows the front clamp in place while **Photo 7.2** shows the rear and the two cross slide screws. The clamp bodies are attached to the saddle, and are in contact with the upper surface of the bed. Simply simply pulling up a lower plate, which then bears on the underside of the bed and the body of the clamp, effects the clamping action. **Figs 7.1** and **7.2** show the component details. It may also be seen

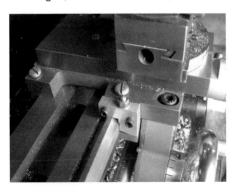

7.1. Front saddle clamp in place, also shows alternative blanking screws.

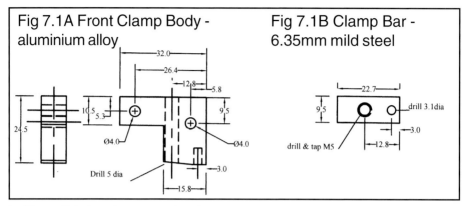

Fig 7.1A Front Clamp Body - aluminium alloy

Fig 7.1B Clamp Bar - 6.35mm mild steel

in **Photo 7.1** that the two socket head grubscrews used to blank the screw positions for the travelling steady have been substituted by a couple of slotted pan head screws. They don't look as neat but it's easier to remove swarf from slots.

Making the clamps is quite straightforward, but before getting started, measure the bed in two places as shown in **Photos 7.3 & 7.4**. What is needed is the vertical thickness, front and back, as the clamps will be made to suit these sizes. It may be observed that the front shear needs to be measured close to the end of the bed, otherwise the rack prevents correct micrometer access. As it is possible that there may be some slight variation between machines, this is best

checked on the individual lathe. The dimensions for other features are generally not critical and are given on the drawings. The thickness chosen was 3/8in. (9.5mm) and this proved quite adequate for the clamping purposes. However when checking later for clearance when used in conjunction with the travelling steady, it was found advantageous to place spacer washers between the front clamp and the saddle. This created space for the clamping nut to turn. A similar result might also be achieved by using thicker material, say 12mm and drilling the 5mm and 3mm holes off centre.

How you go about making the clamps will depend on the equipment available to you. It is possible to produce them entirely with hand tools (hacksaw – file) and a drill, but it may be quicker if you can access a small mill. I sawed off a couple of pieces of 9.5mm aluminium plate, squared them up in the mill (although this be achieved by gripping edgewise in the 4-jaw chuck) and then sawed away the unwanted small rectangle from each, before trimming to size in the mill. The 5mm dia. hole is then drilled

7.2. Rear saddle clamp and cross slide locking screws.

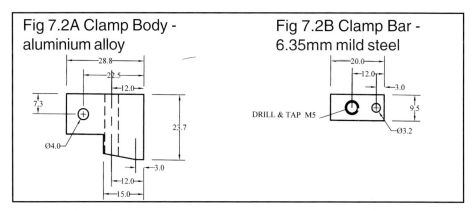

Fig 7.2A Clamp Body - aluminium alloy

Fig 7.2B Clamp Bar - 6.35mm mild steel

centrally on the thickness to leave a 0.5mm wall and the 3mm dia. by 5mm deep hole to accommodate a silver steel anti-rotation pin.

It had been intended that each should be retained by two M4 Allen screws, but after examining the features on the underside of the saddle casting, one only was used on the rear clamp. This has proved satisfactory, so it might be inferred that just one would also suffice at the front. In the case of the prototypes, the 4mm mounting holes were

added, then the lower surface filed away at an angle as can be seen in **Photo 7.5**. This would ensure that when tightened, the load would be applied as in **Fig 7.3**, with the clamp bar bearing correctly against the bed.

This latter component is simply a small piece of steel cut to the dimensions indicated. Note that the prototype for the rear included provision for an adjustment screw, bearing on the clamp body. This proved not to be needed, and the drawings

7.3. Measuring front shear.

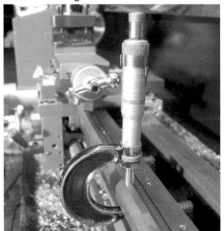

7.4. Measuring rear shear.

7.5. Component parts of the front clamp, note lower surface filed away.

7.6. Rear clamp tightened in position, hard against bed and saddle. (Note only one bolt position used).

for both front and rear reflect the arrangement used at the front. One hole is drilled and tapped M5, the other 1/8in. (clearance for 3mm)

A short length (say 12mm) of 3mm diameter silver steel is cut, de-burred, and fitted to the clamp body with Loctite, the same adhesive being used to hold the clamp bar and M5 screwed rod. In both cases wipe away any excess adhesive which might cause unintended lock up after uniting the two sub assemblies.

Positioning against the saddle

In each case the mounting hole(s) need

to be accurately positioned on the casting. For the rear clamp, first remove the tailstock and move the saddle towards that end of the bed. Engage the half nuts to prevent it sliding towards the headstock. Now fit the rear clamp hard against the bed and the saddle and tighten in position **(Photo 7.6)**. I then used a cordless pistol drill and 4mm drill to spot through the mounting hole. The resulting "spots" can be seen in **Photo 7.7.**

For the front, access is more

7.7. After spotting through with 4mm drill.

Fig 7.3 Clamping Action

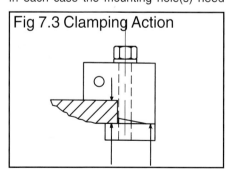

7.8. Transfer punch made from silver steel.

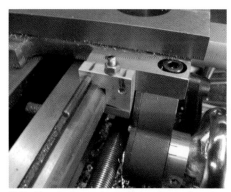

7.9. Front clamp locked in place showing transfer punch.

restricted, and so the pistol drill cannot be used. The easy answer is to make up a silver steel transfer punch. If you have a short length of 4mm diameter, then just grind a point on one end, heat to red-hot and water quench. Otherwise use a piece of slightly larger diameter, and turn down a length of about 13mm to just pass through the 4mm hole, then complete as noted before **(Photo 7.8).** With the clamp locked in place on the bed and against the saddle, the punch can be inserted **(Photo 7.9)** and struck with a small hammer. Note that this time the saddle is restrained by firm hand pressure, as transmitting the force of hammer blows to the half nuts would not be recommended.

After checking for satisfactory indentations, the saddle can then be removed from the lathe, and detached from the cross slide. The saddle casting may then be clamped to an angle plate and the marked positions drilled tapping size for M4. (The generally accepted tapping size is 3.3mm, however experience in production tapping indicated that tap life could be significantly extended

by a small increase in tapping drill diameter. This is a practice I continue to adopt, so here I use a 3.5mm or No 29 drill.) The threads are then tapped.

At this stage, while the saddle is dismantled, you may choose to include the cross slide clamping screw modification described below.

As noted above, the front clamp is assembled being spaced away from the saddle by one M5 washer sandwiched on each mounting screw. This then allows the clamp to be left in situ at times when work on a slender component may require the travelling steady to be fitted.

Cross-slide clamping screws

As supplied, the cross slide is fitted with a gib strip whose adjustment is effected by three screws and locknuts spaced at approximately 55mm. By adding a couple of extra screws as seen earlier in **Photo 7.2**, it is possible to temporarily and quickly tighten up the assembly, in order to undertake milling work, and then afterwards revert to normal.

The cross slide is removed as

discussed previously, then the gib strip taken off. Now determine the height from the lower edge up to the centres of the adjustment screws. It is necessary to mark out and drill the two holes for the new screws at this height (approximately 3mm). Given access to a mill, this may be dealt with by setting up and adjusting the Y position so that a No. 30 drill fitted to the chuck will pass down through the existing holes without deflection, then moving the work along in X to pick up the new.

Without such luxury, the measurements (which can be made before dismantling) might be:

- Thickness of cross slide - approximately 16mm
- Drop from top surface to screw thread – approximately 11mm
- Diameter of screw - nominally 4mm
- From which the centreline is positioned some 13mm from the top surface or 3mm from the underside.

I chose to err a little on the plus side as regards the 3mm figure to be sure of residual wall thickness, and moved the new screws up to about 3.5mm.

The screws are simply a couple of M4 x 20 socket head cap screws, whose ends are modified by filing/ grinding on a cone angle, which will encourage line rather than point contact, when screwed in towards the gib strip.

In Use

As a trial, I clamped a lump of aluminium in the vertical slide, and an 8mm end-mill in the 3-jaw chuck. Note that holding the cutter in this way is not best practice. The collet chuck or a dedicated milling chuck would be preferable, but these may be items that many novices have not yet

acquired. The saddle clamps were then tightened down, and modest pressure applied via the cross slide screws. (Just enough to give a tighter feel to the handle) An initial cut of 0.5mm was followed by one of 1.0mm – the depth being controlled by the leadscrew handwheel. Both cuts were taken at a speed of some 900rpm and engaged the full width of the cutter. The resulting vibration was considered acceptable, although this was considered a severe test for such a small machine, particularly in view of the manufacturer's comment re turning "We recommend that for rough cutting, you do not exceed 0.010in. (0.25mm) as your depth of cut". The 8mm wide trial groove can be seen in **Photo 7.10** and this certainly suggests that much useful milling work will be possible probably using FC3 cutters running at similar or higher speeds.

Parting Off

In the last chapter, I commented on my preference for parting off by means of a rear mounted toolpost, and noted the difficulty which can arise due to deflection, when a front mounted part off tool is used in a lightweight machine. Briefly, a front mounted tool deflects downwards and into the work whereas one at the rear moves up and away. Thus deflection by the front tends to cause dig in whilst at the rear the effect is to reduce the depth of cut. A rear-mounted toolpost would dictate a longer cross slide, and this will be looked at in the longer term. It may also be possible to incorporate modifications to increase the travel of the existing slide. This part of the book looks at an alternative design of part off tool, which involves no modification to the lathe.

Photo 7.11 shows three typical

7.10. Successful trial cutting groove.

7.11. Three commercial part off tools, top 5/8 – 3/4in. middle 1/2in. bottom 5/16in..

conventional parting off tools aimed at larger machines. Each takes a standard HSS blade. **Photo 7.12** illustrates a home made tool employing the same principles. If mounted in a front position, then the comments above apply. **Photo 7.13** illustrates a tool made and kindly presented to me by Ivor Hill who has designed the body so that any flexing will result in movement away from the job. Thus this type of tool can be used to good

effect in a front tool-post.

Two of the features of the C3 Mini-Lathe relevant to this topic, are a) the chuck is retained by three studs and nuts as opposed to a screw on fitting and b) the spindle control incorporates variable speed and forward/reverse facility. The combination of these features means that suitably tooled, you can actually undertake machining work with the lathe running backwards, and the chuck will not unscrew.

7.12. Home made tool to take 5/16in. blade.

7.13. Chatter free tool from Ivor Hill.

7.14. Reverse tool – blade side.

7.15. Reverse tool – mounting side.

Taking advantage of these attributes, we can consider a part off tool set up in the front position, but inverted, and thus arranged to cut in reverse. **Photos 7.14 & 7.15** show two views of the prototype tool, described here, which uses a standard 5/16in. HSS blade, and which is designed to be made with minimal equipment.

Just three components need to be manufactured, as illustrated in **Figs 7.4a, 7.4b** and **7.4c**. These can be produced either with just a drilling machine and hand tools, or using the C3 with the milling sub table described in the previous chapter, to accurately position holes. The standard fasteners needed are two M4 x 20 plus one M5 x 20 socket head cap screws, two M4 x 10 socket head countersunk and one M5 nut and washer.

Before starting, purchase one or two 8mm part off blades such as those supplied by Arc, stock No. 060-320-00940 and measure them. (I have suggested more than one, as in the past I have found it useful to have one blade ground back to a specific width for cutting narrow grooves). Depending on the manufacturer, the thicknesses and angles may vary a little,

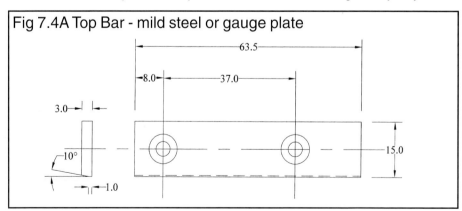

Fig 7.4A Top Bar - mild steel or gauge plate

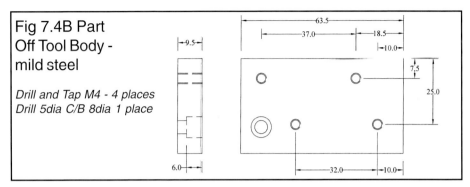

Fig 7.4B Part Off Tool Body - mild steel

Drill and Tap M4 - 4 places
Drill 5dia C/B 8dia 1 place

but in general the form of the cross section will be as shown in **Fig 7.5**, and the thickness at the wider edge will be around 1.5mm and about 1mm at the narrower.

Top Plate and Body

The top and bottom edges of the blade are angled at around 10 degrees, and on this basis, we may progress to make the top plate. A 63.5mm length of bright steel flat or gauge plate 15mm x 3mm is needed. I happened to have gauge plate available, and this would give better wearing properties, particularly if hardened and tempered. It was placed in the vice, and

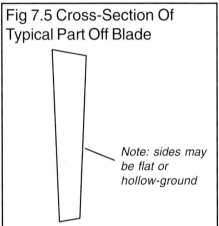

Fig 7.5 Cross-Section Of Typical Part Off Blade

Note: sides may be flat or hollow-ground

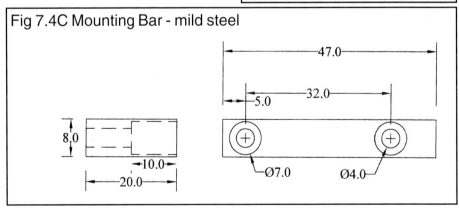

Fig 7.4C Mounting Bar - mild steel

Above: 7.16. Top bar and body showing position of shim. Right: 7.17. Reducing the head diameter.

one edge chamfered by filing at an angle to roughly match the blade. The chamfer was taken a little more than halfway across the 3mm thickness. Progress can be monitored by observing how far across the thickness the chamfer extends. Then mark out, drill and countersink the two 4mm diameter holes.

Work then moved to the body, cutting a rectangle of 3/8in. thick steel plate to 63.5mm x 35mm. You may then choose to clamp the top plate in position and spot through the two holes, or pitch them accurately on the machine. These are then tapped M4. The other two M4 holes may also be added.

Next a piece of 0.010in. (0.25mm) shim is cut 63.5mm long by 8mm wide. The top plate is then assembled to the body by two M4 countersunk Allen screws, trapping the shim as shown in **Photo 7.16**.

The blade is then placed in position resting on the shim and against the top plate. The purpose of the shim is to tilt the blade slightly ensuring that clearance will exist on both sides when in use. (Some cheaper commercial tools are less than perfect in this respect.)

It is now possible to determine the position of the hole for the clamp bolt. This is done by spotting with a 6mm diameter

7.18. Clamp bolt after modification.

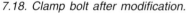

7.19. Mounting bar showing counterbores.

drill just touching the edge of the blade. The hole is then drilled 5mm and counterbored using an 8mm drill to a depth of 5mm.

Clamp Bolt

This starts life as one of the M4 x 20 Allen screws, which then undergoes two modifications. First turn down the head diameter **(Photo 7.17)** to be a snug fit in the counterbore in the body (about 7.98mm if your 8mm drill cuts to size). Next file a flat on the head aiming to achieve an angle to match that on the blade, as shown in **Photo 7.18**. Try the bolt for size. What is needed, is for the head to enter the counterbore (but not bottom in it) before locking on the blade. This way, the clamping load is transferred directly across the head rather than by bending the threaded portion.

Support

This was produced from a 47mm length of 20mm x 8mm bright steel flat. Two holes are drilled through 4mm and countersunk 7mm x 10mm deep **(Photo 7.19)**. Careful positioning is needed here to ensure that the counterbores do not break out. Two alternatives may be considered. The support may be attached by countersunk screws. In this case, the threads are tapped in the support, and holes drilled through the body then countersunk to ensure that the screw heads are under flush to clear the blade. Bar material such as 12mm square would be equally applicable, the component position being arranged by using the lower edge as a datum

Assembly and set up

With the top bar and shim in place, the support is bolted to the back face, and the

7.20. Detached slice can be seen on the cross slide.

blade then located using the clamp screw and nut. As we are working "back to front" it will probably be necessary to grind the end of the blade. My preference is to take off just sufficient material to give a flat "top" surface, then a 90degree (plan view) front. *(In production work, part off tools are often ground with an angled tip so that any pip is left mainly on the stock bar rather than the component just completed. However such geometry introduces side loads. These do not generally cause problems with heavy duty industrial tooling, but at the miniature level, can cause the tool to progress inwards at something other than 90degrees to the axis.)* It may be found easier to grind the blade in the holder, as

• This gives a bit more to hold on to, and

7.21. Slices of mild steel parted off.

- The holder offers rectilinear reference surfaces.

The holder is then set up in the toolpost, shimming/adjusting to ensure that two criteria are met. The end of the blade should be at centre height, and when in position, the blade should lie at 90degrees to the spindle axis viewed from above.

In Use

As a quick trial, a redundant aluminium standoff was gripped in the 3-jaw chuck chuck. **Photo 7.20** shows the part off tool in place; also the short piece sliced away can be seen resting on the cross slide. This really was knife through butter stuff, and a second trial employed a piece of 9.5mm diameter steel. This time there was a little audible vibration, but of course no tendency to dig in and thin slices were taken off with no difficulty. The front/rear faces of two of these can be seen in **Photo 7.21**.

It is quite possible that the tool's performance might be improved by careful attention to the "top" rake, where I have simply used zero degrees, also by using a mounting bar of more robust section such as 12mm square mentioned earlier.

Chapter 8

Guided Centre Punch, Filing Rest, Use of Steadies and Chuck Depth Stop

The comment was made in an earlier chapter that this is a machine often likely to be purchased as a first foray into the world of model engineering or perhaps as the first significant machine tool in the pursuit of related hobbies such as model boats or aircraft. As such, versatility of the machine assumes much greater importance for these owners than for the old hands, who have access to multiple machines and numerous related accessories acquired or made over many years. This article will introduce three further gadgets with this philosophy in mind. In addition, a short description will be given on the use of the fixed and travelling steadies, which are available from the suppliers as accessories for the lathe.

Guided Centre Punch

If making model components such as cylinder end covers or miniature pipe flanges, it will be necessary to mark out and drill the ring of holes for the retaining bolts. This simple gadget, used in conjunction with the headstock dividing attachment described earlier in chapter 5, offers a means of marking out with good accuracy. It consists of just two parts, body,

8.1. The assembled guided punch.

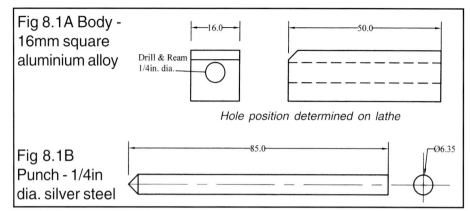

Fig 8.1A Body - 16mm square aluminium alloy

|←16.0→|

50.0

Drill & Ream 1/4in. dia.

Hole position determined on lathe

Fig 8.1B Punch - 1/4in dia. silver steel

85.0

Ø6.35

and punch. I have suggested 1/4in. (6.35mm) diameter silver steel for the punch, but 6mm would be equally suitable. Just modify the design shown in **Figs 8.1A** and **8.1B** to suit. **Photo 8.1** shows the two parts of this simple gadget assembled.

Body

To make the body, take a length of about 50mm of 16mm square section aluminium, and file the top face lightly to that it will fit comfortably in the four way toolpost. File the two ends square, and apply a generous chamfer to one top edge

to identify it as being nearer the headstock. Clamp the block in the toolpost and move the cross slide to bring the centre of the block close to the spindle centreline. Clamp the cross slide using the screws added in part 5 and fit a centre drill to the chuck. Move the saddle towards the chuck to start the hole **(Photo 8.2)**. Change the drill for a 15/64in. or 6mm dia and drill through the length of the body. As can be seen from **Photo 8.3**, I placed a block of wood between the tailstock and toolpost and applied pressure using the tailstock feed screw. Next fit a 1/4in. reamer **(Photo**

8.3. Applying pressure from the tailstock using a wooden block.

8.2 . Hole started with centre drill.

8.4. *Reaming to size.*

8.5. *The point was cut with a part off tool, not particularly recommended but happened to be convenient.*

8.4) and run this through at low speed (100 rpm or less) using plenty of oil. Note that in both the drilling and reaming operations, it will be necessary to draw back repeatedly to clear swarf. (If you have not yet purchased reamers, do not despair, if after drilling through as described, you now drill with a 1/4in. drill, then the hole will be close to size. One of the main reasons which causes a drill to cut oversize is due to the point being ground off centre giving unequal lips. If such a drill is used on virgin metal, then it rotates about its point, and the diameter of the hole is determined by the radius swept by the longer lip. If however a pilot hole has been drilled, then this tendency is reduced and the resulting hole will be nearer to size.)

It will be apparent that by undertaking this drilling operation on the machine, the hole is automatically positioned at centre height.)

Punch

The piece of silver steel was cut to length then chucked to turn a sharp point. As can

8.6. *After hardening, the point was given a lick with a diamond hone.*

be seen in **Photo 8.5,** I did this in an unconventional manner by (ab)using the part off tool described in the last article, which happened to be fitted at the time. The workpiece was then removed from the lathe and the pointed end heated to red heat and water quenched. Immersing the rod vertically will help avoid distortion. The work may then be tempered at around 240deg C (colour pale straw - dark straw).

The point should then be given a final sharpening touch by gripping in the chuck, running up to say 800rpm, and rubbing with a diamond hone or slip stone **(Photo 8.6)**.

8.7. Filing rest fitted to lathe.

Operation

In use, the point of the punch may first be lined up with either a centre which may be either gripped in the chuck or located in the spindle Morse taper, or with the measured periphery or other feature of the work with a known position. The punch may then be taken to a specified radius by moving the cross slide. The workpiece is then indexed by spindle rotation, this being controlled by the dividing accessory. The punch may then be lightly struck to mark positions for drilling.

Filing Rest

This is one of those accessories that more experienced and better equipped enthusiasts may choose to ignore, as they will probably have access to a mill with perhaps dividing head and rotary table.

However, even if you do enjoy such luxuries, for small components, such as miniature hexagon or "D" bolts or a square section for clock winding, then, since we are not planning to remove vast amounts of metal, it can be quicker to produce the form by filing in the lathe. Again, we can use the headstock dividing attachment to set the angular position of the work, so it then remains only to provide means of guiding a file to yield a flat surface in an adjustable and repeatable position.

Filing rests or jigs are not new, and various designs have appeared in the past from authors such as L H Sparey, E T Westbury, and more recently Tony Jeffree. The underlying principle is to provide a pair of hardened rollers whose height may be adjusted, to serve as a depth stop for the file. In this offering, the rollers also feature flanges, so that the sideways progress of the file towards the headstock may be limited. Height is controlled by a graduated wheel on an M12 x 1 thread. Ten major and forty minor divisions are suggested, the latter corresponding to movement of 0.025mm or about 0.001in.

The angular position of the cradle assembly (viewed in plan) may be adjusted, and this feature might be used to file teeth on home made cutters.

The design given here is an adaptation of one constructed earlier for use on a Myford S7, and re-uses some components, although some of the recyclable items have been re-made for the purpose of illustration. The finished unit is shown fitted to the lathe in **Photo 8.7**.

Construction
1. Cradle base (Fig 8.2)
A length of 20mm x 8mm bright steel flat

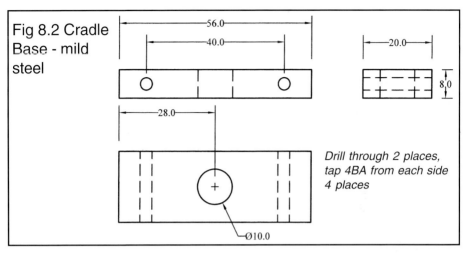

Fig 8.2 Cradle Base - mild steel

Drill through 2 places, tap 4BA from each side 4 places

Ø10.0

bar is cut to a little in excess of the 56mm required. It is then gripped in the 4-jaw chuck chuck and the ends faced to give the correct length. The positions for the three holes are then marked out and these drilled. No great accuracy is needed, however, using the milling table described in an earlier article, would remove some of the guesswork. The 10mm hole might be reamed, but using the technique noted before, if it is drilled 9.5mm then 10mm, it should be close to size. In any case, the mating component will be turned to fit. The other two holes are drilled through the 20mm thickness then tapped 4BA from each side. As the depth is over six times the drill diameter (3mm) repeated pecking is needed to clear the swarf.

2. Cradle side plates (Fig 8.3)
These are made from 3mm thick mild steel sheet, starting with two rectangles 56mm x 30mm. One is clamped to the cradle base, lower edges aligned, and the two bolt holes spotted using the 3mm drill. The positions of the other two holes are

then marked out. The two plates are then clamped together having identified inner/outer faces, and the four holes drilled – two at 3.7mm to take the 4BA bolts, and the upper pair 4mm as tapping size for 2BA. In one plate, this pair of holes is then opened out to 3/16in. For convenience, you may wish to drill the first set of holes then fit these with

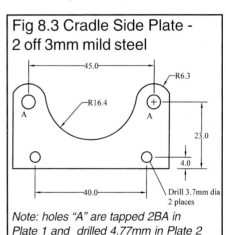

Fig 8.3 Cradle Side Plate - 2 off 3mm mild steel

Note: holes "A" are tapped 2BA in Plate 1 and drilled 4.77mm in Plate 2

Left: 8.8. Side plates for filing rest.
Above: 8.9. Rollers and pins.

4BA bolts to hold the plates together.

The waste material is then cut away from the profile using whatever means you prefer. My method was a combination of bandsaw, hacksaw and file. Note that although radii are dimensioned on the drawing, no accuracy is needed, as we are simply providing clearance for larger diameter work. The completed plates are shown in **Photo 8.8**.

3. Rollers (Fig 8.4A)

This is a straightforward turning job, using silver steel, which is then hardened by heating to "Cherry red" and quenching in water or oil. If quenched in oil, it will probably be necessary to run the 3/16in. drill or reamer through to take off the black deposit.

4 . Pins (Fig 8.4B)

These are also made from silver steel . My procedure was to make the pins over length by several mm, then trial assemble and cut/file off the excess at each end. After cutting the thread with a 2BA die, it will be found that a significant burr is raised at the end of the thread, which must be gently filed off to allow the pin to pass through the first plate and roller. A screwdriver slot is added using a junior hacksaw. After completion and trial assembly, the pins may also be hardened. The two rollers and

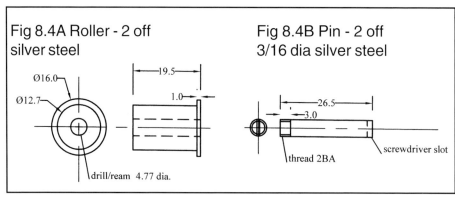

Fig 8.4A Roller - 2 off
silver steel

Ø16.0
Ø12.7
19.5
1.0
drill/ream 4.77 dia.

Fig 8.4B Pin - 2 off
3/16 dia silver steel

26.5
3.0
thread 2BA
screwdriver slot

Fig 8.5 Adjuster Wheel - brass

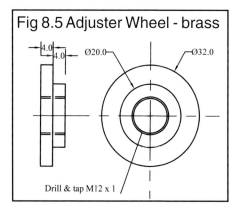

8.10. Adjuster wheel turned and tapped.

associated pins may be seen in **Photo 8.9.**

5. Adjuster wheel and nut (Fig 8.5)

The nut is mentioned only as it can just be seen later in **Photo 14**, where it served to lock the wheel on to the pillar for graduating. A plain spacer would probably suffice, the wheel then being tightened back against the chuck. The wheel is made from a short "cheese" of 32mm brass bar. A 20mm dia spigot is then turned so that it may be reversed and gripped in the 3-jaw chuck for facing, after which it is drilled through 11mm diameter, then tapped M12 x 1mm pitch. As these operations have been dealt

with at one setting, the face of the wheel should run true to the thread, allowing accurate height control. At this stage **(Photo 8.10)** it is placed to one side for added work later.

6. Pillar (Fig 8.6)

A length of 12mm diameter BMS bar is faced to length and centred at one end. This end is then reduced to 10mm diameter for a length of 8mm, aiming for a snug fit in the cradle base. The next 6mm was then reduced to 11m diameter. This feature was intended as a depth guide

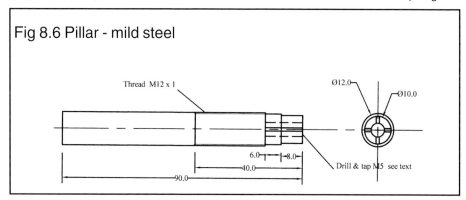

when screwcutting and may be omitted. The work is then drawn out of the chuck sufficiently to allow the screwcutting operation, and supported by the tailstock. I used a sharp pointed 60 degree HSS tool, which required a few thou more than the theoretical infeed. In this situation, I prefer HSS to carbide here, as it is more tolerant of my technique. The half nuts remain closed during the entire operation. First cut is 0.005in deep (five divisions on the cross slide scale), using a low speed of about 60rpm. As the tool approaches the mark (felt tip pen), the spindle is stopped, then the chuck rotated by hand to the desired end point. The tool is then

wound back, and here there would be a risk of breaking a carbide tip. The machine is then reversed, and the procedure repeated. Once the tool starts to graze the 11mm diameter the adjuster wheel can be tried for fit **(Photo 8.11)**. Aim to be able to run the wheel smoothly over the length of the thread without slop. Once you get to a tight fit, it's worth using a thread chaser file to round the crests of the threads.

The end is then drilled about 16mm deep and tapped M5 using only a taper tap. Tap sufficiently deep to allow a 10mm long grubscrew to be screwed in about 6mm. The end is then given four slots some 14mm long, by sawing down with a hacksaw. On assembly, the action of the grubscrew in the tapered thread will give a wedging action, expanding the pillar end, locking the parts together. The final job here is to file a lengthways flat perhaps 4 or 5mm wide on which the clamping screw will act. **Photo 8.12** shows the pillar, and illustrates that due to using a sharp pointed tool, the thread has been cut below the theoretical core diameter.

The pillar is then used as an arbor to carry the adjuster wheel which is first given

Above Left: 8.11. The adjuster wheel is tried for size on the thread. Left: 8.12. Completed pillar.

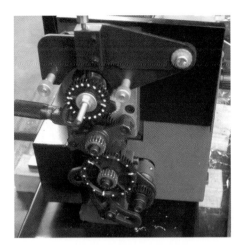

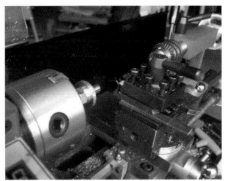

Left: 8.13. Lathe unplugged and dividing attachment fitted. Above: 8.14. Incising the wheel divisions.

a light skim on the OD, then with the power off, the dividing attachment is fitted **(Photo 8.13)**. The saddle stop is set, then the graduations incised, using a vee tool mounted on its side, and racking the saddle back and forth as detailed in an earlier chapter **(Photo 8.14)**. Initially the ten major divisions are marked across the full 4mm width, after which the topslide is wound back about 2mm and the intermediate minor divisions completed. As before, the division marks were coated

with acrylic paint, then wiped after partially drying. **Photo 8.15** shows the pillar assembled with wheel and cradle base.

7. Pillar block (Fig 8.7)

In a similar manner to the cradle base, a piece of 20mm x 30mm BMS bar is sawn and squared up in the four jar chuck. It is then removed, and the position of the 12mm hole marked. The work is then re chucked and offset to centre this feature. As this is a small machine, the drilling procedure I would suggest employs the

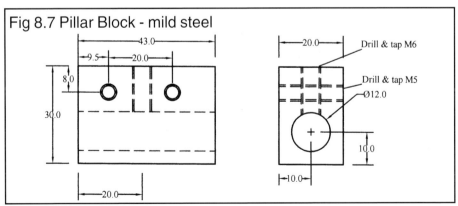

8.15. Pillar assembled with adjuster wheel and cradle base.

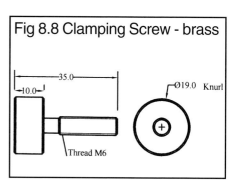

Fig 8.8 Clamping Screw - brass

35.0
10.0
Ø19.0 Knurl
Thread M6

following drills – centre, 8mm, 11.5mm and finally 12mm. The three further holes are then drilled 5mm diameter that for the clamping screw then being tapped M6.

8. Clamping screw (Fig 8.8)

I am suggesting a brass clamping screw for a couple of reasons: first it won't rust, and second, the softer brass will not bruise the surface of the pillar. The design given is turned from a length of 19mm dia. brass rod, the head being knurled, and the thread cut with a M6 die. Other solutions are equally possible, such as a length of M6 screwed rod on to which a tapped head is screwed and retained by Loctite, or even a conventional M6 Allen screw acting via a

brass pad. **Photo 8.16** shows the pillar block with clamping screw.

9. Angle bracket (Fig 8.9)

This part is simply made from a 66mm length of 40 x 40 x 5mm angle smoothed off and drilled. To ensure that the parts fit together, the two 5mm holes may be spotted through from the pillar block.

10. Base clamp (Fig 8.10)

The final component is nothing more complicated than a short piece of 20 x 8 BMS flat, drilled and tapped for an M6 Allen screw, with the corners lopped off at about 45 degrees. Taking off the corners allows the bar to swing round into position when being fitted. The clamp with its associated

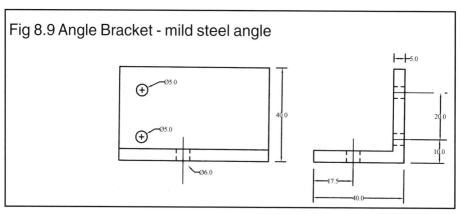

Fig 8.9 Angle Bracket - mild steel angle

Ø5.0
Ø5.0
Ø6.0
40.0
5.0
20.0
10.0
17.5
40.0

Allen screw may be seen in **Photo 8.17**.The assembled rest is illustrated in **Photo 8.18**.

Fixed and travelling steadies

Two steadies are available for the mini lathe, the fixed, which clamps in position on the bed, and the travelling, which is attached to the saddle by means of two bolts, and then moves with it, maintaining a positional relationship with the turning tool.

Above Left: 8.16. Pillar block with clamping screw. Above: 8.17. Base clamp and screw. Below: 8.18. Assembled filing rest shown off the machine.

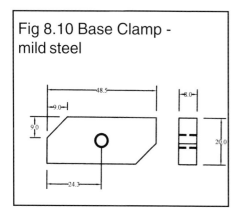

Fig 8.10 Base Clamp - mild steel

8.19. *Fixed steady positioned close to chuck for setting.*

8.20. *Travelling steady in use, note that the tool lags behind the steady.*

The purpose of a steady is to provide the workpiece with added support, which may be needed because the work is long and slender (hence flexible) and cannot gain adequate support from chuck and tailstock.

The fixed steady is equipped with three fingers whose radial position may be adjusted using the screw adjusters, then clamped in place. Ideally setting should be carried out using a short piece of bar whose diameter matches the work. The bar is mounted in the 3-jaw chuck, and the steady positioned on the bed close to the chuck **(Photo 8.19)**. The three fingers are then adjusted to make light contact with the work and locked in position. The steady should then be set correctly for the work in hand.

The travelling steady has just two fingers; positioned to resist the forces (upwards and away) generated at the turning tool. Setting the tool is ideally accomplished in the same manner as before. The travelling steady functions in a similar manner to the roller box often used on industrial capstan lathes. Here the steadying action was applied by small rollers acting on the work. With both the roller box and the travelling steady, two arrangements are possible. The steady may bear on the major diameter of the work, leading the cutting tool, which then turns a smaller diameter. This set up is shown in **Photo 8.20**. Alternatively, the steady may be set to lag slight behind the tool, when the steady must be set for this smaller diameter. This latter arrangement is less likely to be applied in our hobby work, and may require preparatory work on the bar end before starting the cut.

Should it not be possible to do a dummy set up close to the chuck, then it is a case of setting the job in place and progressively adjusting the fingers to achieve on centre running.

Chuck depth stop

If a job requires a number of parts to be made to an identical length, then a depth stop will allow each component to be inserted into the chuck to a repeatable position. Earlier in the series, the headstock dividing attachment was described, the first component being the expanding arbor. This same item may also

8.21. Component parts of chuck depth stop

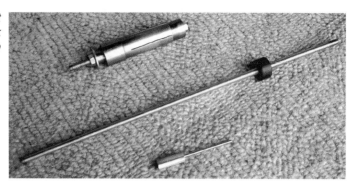

be used as the basis of a simple and effective chuck stop, needing only the addition of a length of studding, steady bush and perhaps special end fittings for small diameter work. **Photo 8.21** shows the expanding arbor along with the added parts, the main item being a 320mm length of M6 screwed rod with a screw driver slot added at one end. Here the steady bush has been made from a piece of black nylon, turned to fit easily in the headstock spindle bore, and tapped M6 to run on the rod. Many other materials would suffice, even wood or MDF. For work in excess of 6mm diameter, the rod can be used without an end fitting however for smaller work something along the lines of that shown, which caters for work down to just over 3mm diameter, may be needed. Here a 25mm length of 8mm AF hex steel bar has been drilled and tapped M6 by 10mm deep at one end, and drilled 3mm diameter by 10mm deep at the other. A 55mm length of 3mm silver steel is then Loctited in place.

Other variations on the depth stop theme have been published over the years, some of which make use of the Morse taper location in the spindle. Stan Bray offers such an arrangement in his book "The Compact Lathe" published by S.I. Model Books.

Chapter 9

Toolpost Powered Spindle, Saw Table and Grinding Rest

Back in the late 1970's, when first setting out in hobby engineering, the two machines in my own shop were an incomplete and cobbled together Herbert drill, and a Myford ML7 lathe. A little later, one of the lots on offer at a club "bring and buy" sale during 1979, was a kit of parts for a toolpost grinding/milling attachment, designed for use on the Myford. After this device was built, it saw a good deal of use until a milling machine was acquired, and even afterwards proved its worth on small work more easily handled in the lathe. As can be seen from **Photo 9.1**, this device is pretty robust and features an on board sewing machine motor and several speeds selected via a multi pulley arrangement. It can be moved by a limited amount vertically before clamping up on the pillar. Note that it may be rotated around the toolpost bolt, but has no provision for angular adjustment in the vertical plane.

Prior to the availability of small electric motors, amateur toolpost devices would frequently be belt driven from an overhead shaft. Such arrangements are in fact, still favoured by many, in particular those using classical ornamental turning equipment within that branch of the hobby.

In the intervening years, new products like the various ranges of mini tools have become available, such as that offered by Arc Euro Trade. These frequently also feature an optional flexi drive and dental style hand piece, which enables the motor unit to be mounted remotely from the tool. My thinking here is to emulate some of the attributes of the earlier toolpost device by means of a simple bracket holding the hand piece, so that it may then be used for light drilling, grinding or cutting operations on work held in the chuck. Alternatively, with the facility for vertical angle adjustment, it might be to sharpen end mills and drills,

9.01. Milling attachment for Myford.

9.02. Mini tool and flexi drive from Aldi.

which would be accommodated in the spindle chuck. Many suitable mini power tools are available from tool stores and DIY chains **(Photo 9.2)**, together with a pack of accessories **(Photo 9.3)**, so work progressed using this kit as a basis. No doubt there will be detail differences between mini tool hand pieces, so my suggestion is to review the concept, examine the equipment to hand then modify to suit.

Construction

1. Bracket

The requirement was simply to create an angle bracket which would allow the hand piece to be raised, lowered, and adjusted for angular position. I chose to achieve this by means of two parts, the base and the slotted upright, both being made from aluminium. Many other arrangements are possible probably determined by whatever you happen to have in your raw material store.

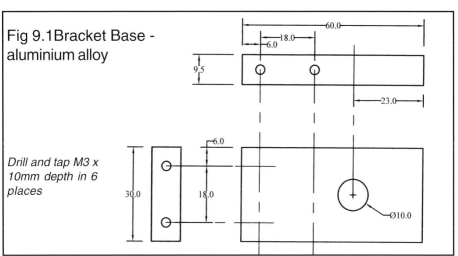

Fig 9.1 Bracket Base -
aluminium alloy

Drill and tap M3 x
10mm depth in 6
places

9.03. The matching accessory pack.

9.04. Base at this stage has one pair of mounting holes.

2. Bracket Base

A suitable piece of aluminium flat bar 9.5mm thick was cut and to the rectangular shape as shown in **Fig 9.1**. The single 10mm dia hole was then drilled, followed by the three pairs at 2.5mm dia. which were then tapped M3.

Initially just one pair of M3 were provided on the end face, **(Photo 9.4)** however once set up on the machine it was clear that adding alternative mounting positions for the slotted upright would improve the versatility of the device.

3. Bracket Upright

The material chosen here is 1in x 3/16in. aluminium flat, cut to a length of about 102mm as shown in **Fig 9.2**. The two M3 holes are drilled at 18mm pitch to match

the base. It will depend on your equipment how you chose to deal with this. For enthusiast with fairly basic kit, it may be advantageous to produce this part first, then spot through on to the sides of the base. One beneficial modification would be to use countersunk screws, in which case, the 4mm step in the toolholder might be omitted.

My preferred method for cutting the 5mm slot employed a 3/16in. dia FC3 "throwaway" cutter. These cutters can be used as slot drills, i.e. they can be driven in just as a drill, so step one was to rough out the slot by a sort of chain drilling technique, stepping across about 1.5mm between cuts. The cutter may then be set to about half depth and run down the

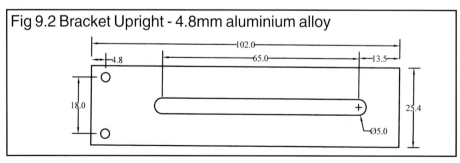

Fig 9.2 Bracket Upright - 4.8mm aluminium alloy

Above: 9.05. The completed upright. Below: 9.06. MDF toolholder with screwed rods glued in place.

length of the slot. This is then repeated at full depth. The work is then moved sideways a little over 0.1mm and a cut taken to widen the slot. The final cut on the other face is taken at a depth to give the required 5mm width. Note that when working along the slot you should ensure that the direction of feed opposes the rotation of the cutter. If this is not the case, then "climb milling" results. Where backlash exists in the feed screw, it is possible for the work to be drawn in to the cutter with adverse results. The completed upright is illustrated in **Photo 9.5**.

4. Tool holder

This item was actually made twice. Mark 1 was a simple rectangular block but interference with the heads of the two M3 screws limited downwards movement, so the redesigned Mark 2 is shown in **Fig 9.3**. The modifications are:

• M5 screwed rod serves the dual purposes of retaining the holder and clamping the tool and

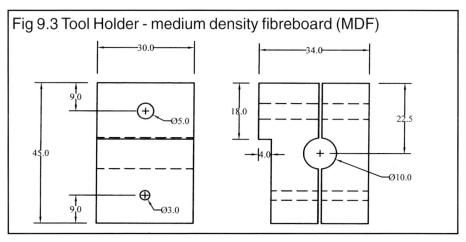

Fig 9.3 Tool Holder - medium density fibreboard (MDF)

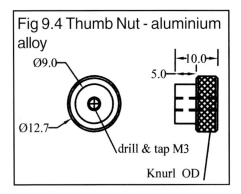

Fig 9.4 Thumb Nut - aluminium alloy

Ø9.0
5.0
10.0

Ø12.7
drill & tap M3
Knurl OD

9.07. A pair of aluminium thumbnuts.

- The 4mm step.

Together they avoid the problem and permit the tool to be set lower down with reference to the slot.

I used a section of 30mm thick MDF was cut to a rectangular shape, then drilled through 1/2in. (tool location), then 5mm and 3mm in for the clamping studs. The 4mm step was then sawn out, after which the piece was cut in two by sawing diametrically across the 1/2in. hole. The sides of the location postion were then opened out slightly by filing to improve the fit on the handpiece body.

Araldite was then employed to fix in place the M5 and M3 screwed rods, which had been cut to lengths of 55mm and 40mm respectively

giving the result shown in **Photo 9.6**.

5. Thumb Nut and Toolpost Nut

For the Mark 1 tool holder, two aluminium thumbnuts were made shown in **Photo 9.7** and detailed in **Fig 9.4.** For Mark 2, only one nut is used, but we now work with two standard M5 nuts and washers. The thumb nut is a straightforward turning job and needs little comment. Eagle eyed readers may deduce that the tool post nut shown is actually made from 5/8in. AF hex bar, however **Fig 9.5** specifies 17mm AF as this size will fit a spanner which is already present in the Mini Lathe toolkit. Again a regular turning job, note though that the nut **(Photo 9.8)** is counterbored

9.08. Toolpost nut.

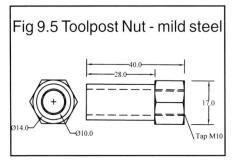

Fig 9.5 Toolpost Nut - mild steel

40.0
28.0
17.0
Ø14.0
Ø10.0
Tap M10

Left: 9.09. Hand piece, flexi drive and power unit mounted. Below Left: 9.10. Touching up a 1/8in. drill. Below Right: 9.11. The hardware removed from the machine.

10mm dia to reduce the amount of thread engagement and expedite fitting to and removal from the machine.

Use

Photo 9.9 shows the hand piece and bracket mounted on the topslide, with the Mini tool power unit located on its pendant. By using a thin grinding disc, and a slow main spindle speed, it becomes possible to cut grooves in, or even part off hard materials.

If power is disconnected from the lathe and the headstock dividing unit fitted, then it becomes a straightforward matter to drill small holes on a pitch circle.

Because the hand piece is mounted

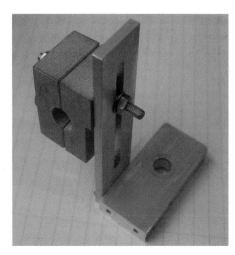

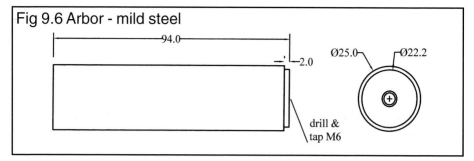

Fig 9.6 Arbor - mild steel

94.0

2.0

Ø25.0

Ø22.2

drill &
tap M6

on the topslide, three movement axes are available: axial, using the leadscrew handwheel, transverse, by means of the cross slide, and angular, determined by the topslide setting. Thus if the topslide is set to move at 59 degrees to the lathe axis, then it is possible to touch up the edges of standard drills (118 deg.) **Photo 9.10** shows this exercise in progress, where the tool is fitted with a thin grinding disc, and is being used to lick the edges of a 1/8in. drill. **Photo 9.11** gives a view of the assembled bracketry off the machine.

2. Saw Table

If you care to examine the range of accessories, which used to be offered by Myford for their Seven series lathes, you will come across a saw table and arbor, intended to accept a 5in. dia. metal cutting slitting saw. I understand that it is no longer available, principally due to the changes in Health and Safety requirements. My proposal here adopts the concept of the Myford device, but uses one of the 115mm dia. diamond discs, which have become available in recent years at ever decreasing prices. These are available in various forms with either segmented or continuous periphery. The latter is used here, as it is thought that the lack of "teeth"

would bring safety considerations broadly into line with those for abrasive discs. Nevertheless we are still setting up an unguarded rotating tool, which will warrant a common sense approach to its use. This table is locked in a horizontal position and hence may be used for cutting and grinding at 90degrees.

Just six components are needed, two from a length of 25mm BMS bar for the arbor, two pieces of 50 x 50 x 5mm steel angle for the mounting brackets, and two pieces of 6mm aluminium plate for the table top. No great precision is needed, except to ensure that the mounting matches the topslide retaining disc, the mounted height clears the top of the arbor,

9.12. Bar supported by fixed steady.

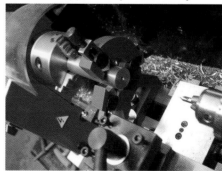

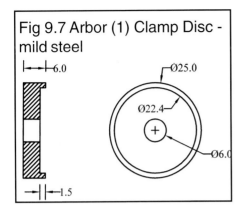

Fig 9.7 Arbor (1) Clamp Disc - mild steel

9.13. Arbor components with diamond disc.

and to maintain the 4mm parallel slot between the table top plates. The diamond disc used here features a bore diameter of 22.2mm, and a thickness of approximately 1mm at the bore and 1.5mm at the periphery. Others were found to be slightly thicker, hence the 4mm slot.

1. Arbor Fig 9.6

A length of 25mm BMS was set up with the fixed steady as shown in **Photo 9.12** then faced to 94mm, centred, and the 22.2mm dia. location spigot formed. It was then drilled and tapped M6 for the retaining screw. The spigot was made rather longer that the thickness of the disc to ensure satisfactory location. This would then entail a mating counter bore in the clamp disc. This simple arrangement worked well because the 3-jaw chuck is new and pretty accurate, hence in use, the arbor and rotates truly with very little swash at the disc periphery. If your chuck is not accurate, then consider other options, which may include: working with the 4-jaw chuck and setting accurately on centre, turning the arbor between centres with a reduced location diameter to match a collet chuck, or starting with a No 3 Morse taper arbor

and drawbar, then adding an extension retained by Loctite.

A further variation would employ a longer arbor, supported at the right hand end by the tailstock. In this case, the disc would be held in place by a suitable fine thread nut. (Tracy Tools list 20 and 22m diameter by 1 and 1.5mm pitch.

Diamond discs feature various bore sizes, so size the arbor spigot accordingly.

2. Clamp disc Fig 9.7

A thin disc of the same bar was sawn off then faced on both sides to 6mm it was then drilled 6mm and counterbored to a little over 22.2mm diameter and a depth of 1.5mm. The arbor components with diamond disc are shown in **Photo 9.13**.

3. Base Bracket Fig 9.8

When the topslide is removed, by unscrewing the two M6 retaining screws, the lower retaining disc is revealed. It is this part that will be used to secure both the saw table assembly, and the grinding rest which follows. The lower disc carries two M6 tapped holes and a protruding peg 8mm in diameter, these features being

Fig 9.8 Base Bracket - mild steel

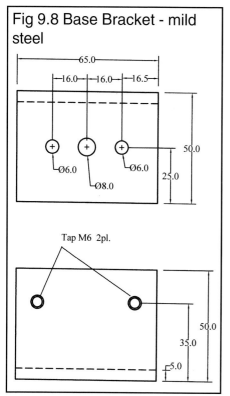

Fig 9.9 Table Bracket - mild steel

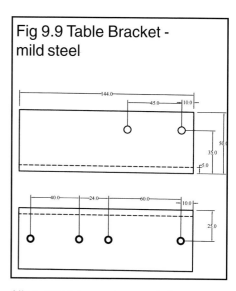

Allen screws can be used, however a couple of washers will be needed on each to accommodate the difference in thickness. Experience in use however suggests that if a couple of hex headed screws are used, then spanner access at final setting will be easier.

4. Table Bracket Fig 9.9

This is also made from another length of the same steel angle, this time 144mm. Let us deal first with the two holes on the vertical face. Positions are detailed on the

spaced on my machine at 16mm centres. Cut a length of 50 x 50 x 5mm steel angle to a length of 65mm and drill the 8mm and 6.35mm location holes. Check for fit on the machine. If there is a bit of interference, just open up the 6.35 holes a little to gain extra clearance. It is possible that thinner section angle would give adequate rigidity, however opting for a thickness of 5mm gives enough meat to give reasonable tapped threads thus avoiding the need for separated fiddly nuts. Note that for fixing the base in place, the original topslide

9.14. View of the two brackets.

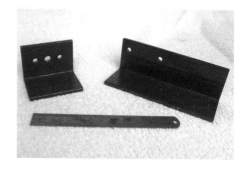

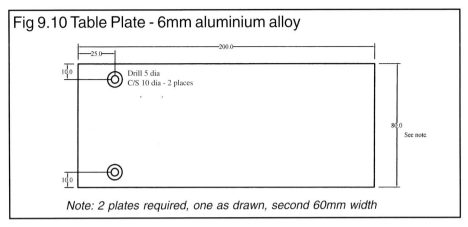

Fig 9.10 Table Plate - 6mm aluminium alloy

Drill 5 dia
C/S 10 dia - 2 places

Note: 2 plates required, one as drawn, second 60mm width

drawings, however it will be quite adequate to clamp these two bracket parts together ensuring 1) that the top and bottom faces are parallel, 2) that the spacing gives clearance over the arbor, and then to drill through 5mm at two approximately correct positions. The holes in the base bracket are then tapped M6, and those in the table bracket opened up to 6mm. **Photo 9.14** illustrates these two brackets.

5. Table Top Plates Fig 9.10 and Photo 9.15
A similar philosophy may be applied to these parts. Hole positions for the screws

attaching top plates to the angle are detailed, but as long as the plates are located at about 90degres to the angle and a 4mm parallel gap is obtained, the actual screw positions are not important. Thus you may choose to clamp together and drill through prior to tapping the steel M5 and opening up and countersinking the aluminium. My box of M5 countersunk screws contained some socket head and some slotted head. It was noted that the slotted typed carried a significant burr on the underside of the head from the (final)

9.15. Two table top plates.

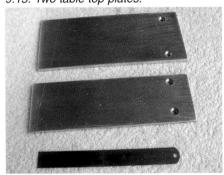

9.16. Saw Table assembled on Mini Lathe.

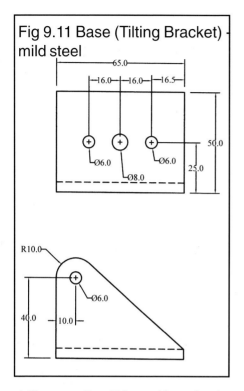

Fig 9.11 Base (Tilting Bracket) - mild steel

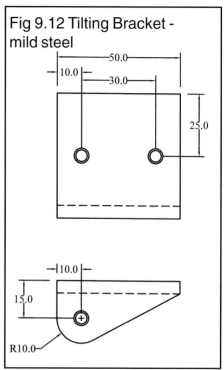

Fig 9.12 Tilting Bracket - mild steel

slotting operation. This would need to be removed before fitting.

The assembled saw table may be seen fitted to the machine in **Photo 9.16**.

Grinding Rest

The general concept here is similar to that for the saw table, but the top plate is a single piece (although offered as two versions) and includes provision for setting at an angle. The arrangement has been kept as simple as possible and hence lacks refinement such as a built in graduated protractor. After setting up for

use with the cheap diamond disc, it occurred that the arrangement might also be used with one of the more expensive diamond wheels, and a second arbor was

9.17. A turned button is used as a filing guide.

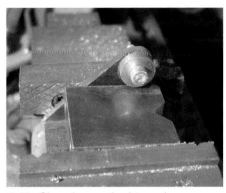

9.18. Clamping method to reduce vibration.

9.20. Cut away top supports work behind the disc face.

duly turned up to accommodate this.

1. Brackets Figs 9.11 and 9.12

These are made as before from short lengths of 50 x 50 x 5mm steel angle, however this time we do not need to go over the arbor, so the mounted height has been reduced, and to allow for angular adjustment, the shape in elevation, has been made triangular with rounded corners.

After cutting to length, drilling and sawing roughly to shape, work proceeded with a file. A turned button held in place by an M6 screw **(Photo 9.17)** served as a guide to get a reasonable looking radius. **Photo 9.18** shows the work clamped in the vice, using a piece of 1/2in. thick flat to grip the work in a way that would improve rigidity and reduce vibration. The completed brackets are shown in **Photo 9.19**.

2. Rest Plates (Tops) Figs 9.13 and 9.14

Again each is made from a rectangle of 6mm aluminium plate, squared off, then drilled and countersunk for the M5 retaining screws. One is a simple square each side being 85mm long. The second

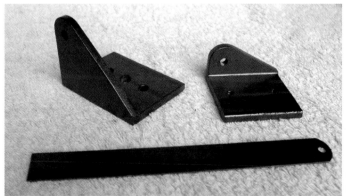

9.19. Two completed brackets.

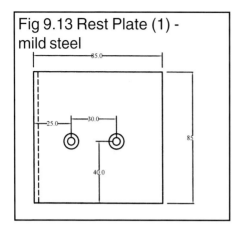

Fig 9.13 Rest Plate (1) - mild steel

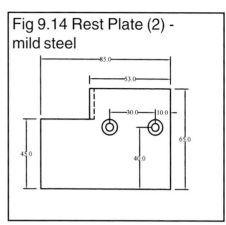

Fig 9.14 Rest Plate (2) - mild steel

has a cut out, which allows the surface to project to the rear of the wheel edge. This allows work such as lathe tools to be supported as shown in **Photo 9.20**. The underside of the edge close to the surface of the disc/wheel has been heavily chamfered (about 3mm) so that the rest top face can be moved that bit nearer the abrasive surface.

3. Arbor (2) Fig 9.15

My diamond cup wheel (obtained some time ago from Eternal Tools) has a bore of 1/2in. and a location thickness in excess of 3/8in. It was therefore decided to use a spigot of about this length working with a plain clamp disc, as depicted in the drawing. In **Photo 9.21** this wheel can be seen mounted on its arbor set up with the cut away rest top. Similar wheels may be obtained from Arc and others. The range supplied by Arc covers a variety of shapes, and diameters both external and internal. Working from their list, my suggestion would be to opt for either the 10 or 20mm bore, adopt as a personal standard, and machine the arbor to suit.

Added Embellishments

These projects have been presented in a basic and simple format in the hope that this will encourage the less experienced to extend the versatility of their machines. In the case of the saw table, it would be straightforward to add a clamp on

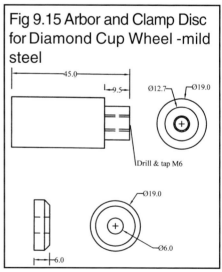

Fig 9.15 Arbor and Clamp Disc for Diamond Cup Wheel -mild steel

adjustable fence, and for the grinding rest, to add guide and clamping details to hold work at predetermined angles. In this arrangement, angle setting is accomplished by means of a protractor held against the disc or wheel and rest top.

Comments after initial applications

The cheap diamond disc proved a little on the coarse side for producing a good tool edge on carbide (although probably better than a green grit wheel). Nevertheless, it offers a useful approach for roughing to shape. Changing to the "Eternal" cup wheel, it became very easy to create a sharp edge with accurately determined clearance angles.

When working on a left-hand tool, if the disc is fitted, then the rear face can be brought into play. Obviously this is not possible with the cup wheel, and this prompted the thought of an extended rest top projecting to the rear of the lathe, and having a rectangular cut out to accommodate the wheel. This would then allow left-handed tools to be supported to the rear of the lathe axis.

It was noted earlier that the grinding debris emanating from a diamond disc or wheel is very much less than from a conventional grinding wheel. However the dust particularly from carbide (and HSS) tools will be very hard and hence potentially abrasive. It is therefore worth introducing some form of guard to keep dust off the bed ways. This might be a modified version of the bed protector outlined earlier in the series, or just a piece of stiff card cut to shape. A piece of rag is not recommended as this can be caught and wound in by the rotating parts.

When these gadgets were first considered, the aims were fairly limited, but included attempting to give the novice an easy approach to tool sharpening. Having enjoyed initial "playtime" sessions with the kit, it occurs that with extra items such as fences, guides, and clamps one could undertake some very effective grinding work. The Mini-Lathe is never going to double up as a "Quorn", but for much of what we want to do, in terms of basic tool shaping and sharpening, this simplistic avenue may be worth more than a second thought.

Chapter 10

DRO Handwheels, Taper Roller Bearings and a Radius Turning Attachment

One of the accessory kits offered for the lathe by Arc is the DRO arrangement for the topslide and cross slide, which take the form of a readout assembly fitted behind each handle. As the readout electronics are "geared" to 20 tpi, the system requires a different screw pitch, and hence the kit includes replacement leadscrews, also the cross slide feed nut, and topslide base, each of which is appropriately tapped. The kit arrives in a

moulded protective expanded polystyrene packing, the individual components being further wrapped and protected **(Photo 10.1)**. Also included is a six-page instruction leaflet, which gives a series of clear captioned pictures.

Critics will point out that these DRO's operate by measuring rotation of the particular screw, hence unlike a slide type readout, they will not correct for backlash so you need to remember to work consistently in one direction. For lathework, unlike milling, it must be said that this is unlikely to be of great significance, since most tools will be operated in one direction. What they will do is first change the screw pitch from 1mm to 20tpi, which means less handle twirling between extremes. Secondly, you will no longer need to count turns and finally you will be able to switch

10.1. The DRO kit showing interior wrapping and protective outer.

10.2. The topslide moving parts have been removed.

10.3. and protractor scale detached.

between imperial and metric readings at the touch of a button.

Cautionary note

If your workshop is like mine, and unheated, all the equipment will be subjected to variations of temperature and humidity, those experienced during the winter months being of particular concern. Notably this winter, my solar powered calculator went completely haywire, and as usual, the digital callipers gave me a low battery signal. The same type of batteries is fitted to the DRO handwheels, and in one case this too had "gone down" in storage. A couple of spares are included with the kit. For cold workshop conditions, it may be worth considering removing the batteries after work to prolong their lives. Battery changing involves removing a couple of small screws to release the compartment cover, fine if you are regularly working on minute parts, but for the more clumsy like me, this is an opportunity to lose screws. An easy alternative would be to fit the battery cover, omit the screws, and apply a piece of

masking or electrical tape as a retainer.

In a similar vein, it must be noted that these DRO units are not proof against the ingress of oil or coolant suds. So if you use coolant, on your C3, then I suggest it be applied sparingly by brush (In any case you do not want it getting into the motor or control electronics.) Flooding with high-pressure coolant as per industrial practice is a definite no. Again, one of my dodges for winterisation of equipment is to spray generously with WD40. Clearly this should not be allowed on the readout surface. I have been told that in one model engineering club, members who use these devices, have come up with a slip on protective cover, which might be made from a thin brass frame and Perspex window.

Topslide conversion

For the Topslide readout conversion, the main stages are as follows

• Slacken the gib screws and wind back the handle until the screw disengages then slide off the upper part of the topslide. Remove the handle and feed screw. **(Photo 10.2)**

10.4. Upper section and scale reassembled on new base.

10.5. The new leadscrew is greased and wound in.

• Remove the protractor scale, **(Photo 10.3)** and transfer to the new base. Remove the two Allen screws holding the topslide base and lift this away, to substitute the replacement.

• Lubricate, then slide the upper section onto the lower dovetail, and adjust the gib screws to allow the slide to be moved by hand but with some resistance. **(Photo 10.4)** Apply Copaslip or similar lubricant to the feed screw then wind this in. **(Photo 10.5)**

• Fit the replacement feed screw retainer, then its two retaining screws. Check that the feedscrew rotates freely as the screws are tightened.

• Slide the DRO head over the screw, then fit a small set screw ensuring that it enters the keyway (shown in **Photo 10.6)** in the feedscrew. Fitting this (for me) tiny M3 grubscrew really had me wishing for smaller fingers, however the technique adopted was to magnetise a small

10.6. Close up showing the keyway.

10.7. A scraper is employed to ease the counterbore.

10.8. Canting the readout head improves clearance.

10.9. Picking up the hole position. Note spacers need to be added to avoid marking chuck.

jeweller's screwdriver, after which engaging the screw proved to be no problem. Next fit the three screws which retain the head. The supplied label may then be applied to hide these screws. Adding the shroud, spacer washer and handle completes the operation.

After fitting the DRO head and its three fixing screws, I encountered a minor problem in that the shroud would not enter its mating counterbore in the head. The second assembly (still in the box) was also checked and found to be the same. The cause may be just the paint applied to

the head, and certainly the solution proved to be quite simple. A scraper was gently worked around the bore, **(Photo 10.7)** and after a couple of minutes, the shroud slipped easily into place. The second head was given the same treatment.

Having fitted the topslide DRO, it was noted that it might be possible for it to foul the tailstock chuck when turning small diameters. An alternative mounting position is therefore proposed, rotating the head 60 degrees towards the operator **(Photo 10.8)**. This brings it back away from the machine centre line and the tailstock chuck. In order to try out the mod quickly, I simply set the mounting bracket up in the mill, on a rotary table. This made it easy to pick up on one of the existing holes, using a 2.5mm drill, **(Photo 10.9)** next to index round 60 degrees then for three positions at 120degrees. Note that **Photo 10.9** was taken before the two parallel spacers visible in **Photo 10.10** were added. The

10.10. Three new positions are spotted and drilled.

10.11. Then tapped ensuring the tap is held perpendicular to the work.

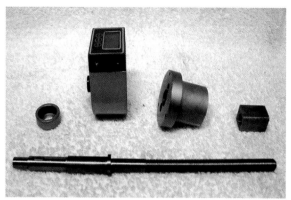

10.12. The new components for the cross slide conversion.

three locations were first spotted with a centre drill before drilling through 2.5mm **(Photo 10.10)** and tapping M3. As mentioned in earlier articles, the tap was kept square to the work by my general purpose tapping guide **(Photo 10.11).** After completion of the work, the bracket was refitted, and the head reassembled, canted over. A secondary advantage of this modification may also be that the battery compartment is now more accessible. This mod could be carried out using the Mini-Lathe to mark out and perhaps drill the holes. This would entail fitting the headstock dividing attachment (60 tooth wheel) and the guided punch, then gripping the bracket very lightly in the 3-jaw chuck. The punch should then be accurately aligned with one of the existing holes, and the chuck tightened. Then index round 60degrees and punch. Repeat for positions 2 and 3 at 120 degree intervals.

10.13. The feed nut is wound on to the screw.

Cross slide conversion

Details of the conversion parts are shown in **Photo 10.12**. For the cross slide, the sequence is generally similar, but starts with the removal of the two capscrews holding the feed nut in place. This is then removed by winding the handle. The existing screw and retainer are then removed, and the new fitted. The feed nut (screw holes facing upwards) is then wound on to the screw **(Photo 10.13),** the two cap screws fitted (but not tightened) to retain it, and then the head and handle

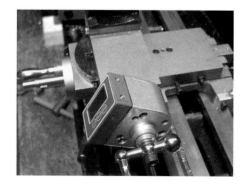

10.14. Rotation may still exceed 30 degrees.

a clear reading of the dial position, the facility to zero at any point, to avoid counting (miscounting) handle turns and to instantly change from imperial to metric readings. On the other hand, as can be seen from **Photo 10.14**, rotation of the topslide is now restricted but still can be moved in excess of 30degrees. Whether this restriction is a cause for concern will depend very much on the type of work undertaken and techniques practised.

Bearing Change

If my understanding of history is correct, the Mini Lathe was based on an earlier Russian designed machine, which featured a headstock fitted with a pair of taper roller bearings. The Chinese manufacturers decided to change the specification of the bearings and employ ball bearings, which fitted the same housing and shaft diameter dimensions. It may be that this was a cost driven modification, or it may be that they considered the maximum spindle speed of about 3000 rpm to be better handled by ball rather than taper roller bearings, which can also generate significant drag if installed with excessive preload.

fitted. A series of steps is given in the instructions to adjust the feed nut. These aim to first set its height to match the leadscrew (using the middle screw jacking downwards), then to eliminate backlash by a slight tilting action induced by the front and rear retaining screws, and are as follows:

• Loosen all three screws

• Wind the cross slide out towards the operator until it contacts the dial.

• Tighten the centre screw until the handle becomes stiff to turn.

• Loosen the centre screw until the feed handle just turns freely.

• Tighten the screw nearest the operator until the handle becomes stiff to turn.

• Slacken the same screw until the handle just turns freely.

• Nip up but do not tighten, the third screw farthest from the operator

After fitting both read out heads, it was felt that these are accessories, which will be very much to the taste of many enthusiasts, but perhaps not all. On one hand, they offer major advantages in giving

For the vast majority of work, the ball races fitted as standard, are quite up to the demands placed upon them, however in the best model engineering traditions of quarts and pint pots, some owners wish to fit bigger chucks and turn heavier chunks of metal. In these situations, the extra load capacity and stiffness offered by taper roller races can convey advantages in terms of reduced vibration and improved finish. From one bearing catalogue it appears

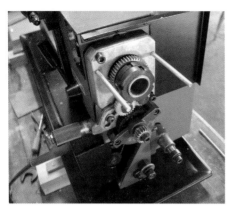

10.15. Change gears removed and tumbler cluster screws slackened.

10.16. Two C spanners used to remove the ring nuts.

that in this instance, the load capacity of the taper roller bearing is about double that of the corresponding ball race.

The procedure is essentially that of unscrewing various parts at the change gear end, releasing the bearing retainer and drawing the main spindle out and over the bed. Note that some modern versions of the Mini Lathe have a speed-sensing disc which must be refitted close to the same axial position (requiring modification to spacers). Earlier machines may not embody this. Due to the TR bearings having a different axial dimension to the originals, after fitment, the spindle will move towards the tailstock by about 1.25mm, and the dimension between the inner faces of the two inner tracks will increase by some 2.5mm. When they undertake bearing conversions, Arc insert a machined spacer (with keyway), however, if the lathe has already been dismantled,

then this requires the use of a second lathe. An alternative approach is therefore proposed which is intended to give the same result but arrived at more easily by the home enthusiast without access to additional machinery.

Photo 10.15 shows an early state of play with the chuck, splashback, change gear cover, and gear train removed. The two Allen screws retaining the tumbler assembly have also been slackened. In

10.17. The control panel detached, the sensor board is still held in place on the headstock.

10.18. Close up showing the slotted opto sensor.

10.19. The sensor disc and spindle spacers can be seen through the aperture.

Photo 10.16, this has also been taken off, and a pair of C spanners is used to release the two ring nuts on the spindle. With these cleared, the steel gear can be removed, (and its key carefully stored). To release the drive pulley, its circlip is removed, after which the belt can be "walked" off the pulley, and the pulley slid off its shaft. This then gives clearance to remove the rear bearing cover after undoing its three Allen screws.

The four screws are then undone, allowing the control panel to be drawn back.

Photo 10.17 shows this and the location of the speed sensor board, which is still fixed to the headstock. This small board can be seen in **Photo 10.18**, the slotted sensor being visible. The aperture in the headstock can be seen in **Photo 10.19**, and through it, the slotted sensor disc.

Attention then turns to the front end of the headstock, and removal of the three screws holding the bearing cover. **(Photo 10.20)** The way is now clear to draw out the spindle. It will depend on the particular

10.20. Three screws are accesses through holes in the flange.

10.21. Components for a "Heath Robinson" puller.

10.22. *The puller in use.*

10.23. *The front bearing has been pulled along the spindle to contact the key.*

fit of your machine as to whether this is easy or difficult. After a couple of perfunctory taps with a mallet, I chose to set up the puller arrangement whose components (M10 screwed rod, square RHS, and aluminium flat) are shown in **Photo 10.21**. **Photo 10.22** shows the thing in use. From **Photo 10.23**, it can be seen that during the exit process, the front bearing was forced along the spindle making contact with, and bruising the nose of the key. **(Photo 10.24)** this minor damage was dressed off with a file.

To remove the bearing from the spindle, Arc recommend the use of a hydraulic press with suitable attachments. Unfortunately no suitable attachments were to hand so two other methods were tried, both successful. The first harks back to my student days in the 60's, when I needed to remove the bearing from a rear halfshaft on a 1936 Singer Le Mans. A trip to the local garage provided the answer. They kept a block of lead especially for such duties, parked in a corner on the floor.

The shaft was simply held vertical and smacked down on the block. After a few whacks, the bearing fell away. My alternative is a block of aluminium **(Photo 10.25)** and, as with the lead, the softer material avoids damage to the spindle end. Alternatively, **Photo 10.26**, shows a gadget knocked up a few years ago which also worked here. It was intended as a spring compressor for suspension struts, the compression being

10.24. *- causing slight bruising to the nose of the key.*

Left: 10.25 Method one – the aluminium block. Above: 10.26 . Method two – a suspension compressor.

applied by two lengths of M16 screwed rod.

It then remains only to dismount the bearing left in the rear of the headstock. Arc use a purpose made gripper and a slide hammer. Whilst I could lay my hands on a slide hammer, a gripper was entirely another matter. I therefore resorted to using a brass drift inserted through the headstock (and the interior parts).

The way was now clear to consider reassembly, and whereas Arc produce and fit a purpose machined spacer, it was thought that for many home workers, it would be easier and equally effective to fit two spacer rings, one immediately inboard of each inner track. Each is easily made from a short length of wire 18g at the front, 0.8mm at the rear. The front is a simple ring made by winding the galvanised soft steel wire around a bar (say about 25mm diameter to allow for spring back). I wound on about three turns, then snipped to size. That for the rear is treated similarly, but

was made from 0.8mm Mig welding wire. After forming to a circle, more bends were applied to give a "wavy" washer effect. The two rings are shown in **Photo 10.27**. Once installed, as the rear bearing is adjusted up, this will then apply pressure to the stack of spacers, gear and sensor disc, bringing them back close to original axial position. One other small mod is suggested by Arc. A small step is turned on the rear end of the rear spacer, to ensure that it clears the cage of the adjacent bearing.

Fitting the new bearings then follows normal practice. Anyone who has changed car wheel bearings will find a familiar scenario. After cleaning the housings, the two outers are fitted to the headstock. I used first a nylon mallet, followed by hammer and brass punch. You can detect when the track has bottomed by the change in sound of the blows.

To push the first inner on to the spindle, you ideally require a length of tube

10.27. The two wire ring spacers.

slightly larger than 30mm bore. My scrap box contained part of a Land Rover hub assembly, which served to do the job. The bearing is then greased, and the spindle, with its long key in place, fed into the headstock. Care is needed to line up the various parts so that they slide over the key **(Photo 10.28).**

The rear spacer may then be added, followed by the rear bearing inner track. I eased this into approximate position, again using the brass drift as a punch, working from side to side. After assembling the outer spacer, key and gear, the first of the ring nuts was screwed on and wound up to push the bearing into position. One point to note here is that the spacer will have moved along the spindle, slightly and therefore can foul the gear key. I chose to file a little off both parts to achieve clearance.

Spindle end float was checked with a clock gauge, **(Photo 10.29),** and the ring nut progressively tightened until no

10.28. Spindle assembly is fed thought the spacer, disc and gear.

10.29. End float is checked with a clock gauge.

movement could be detected. The second nut was then added and the two locked. In this type of arrangement, I back off the first nut a tiny amount to compensate for the change in setting caused by its movement along the thread when the locknut is tightened against it. The spindle was then checked for endfloat and freedom of rotation.

Brief Digression on Taper Roller Bearing Adjustment

Referring to an old copy of an SKF General Catalogue, I came across a paragraph on bearing stiffness, which commented that in most cases this is high enough to be disregarded, but can be of significance in applications such as machine tool spindles. It was then noted that roller bearings have greater stiffness than ball bearings, and that the stiffness can be enhanced by preloading.

I also consulted a couple of car workshop manuals with regard to wheel bearing adjustment. Jaguar in the 1950's recommended endfloat of 0.003 to 0.005in. while in the 80's, Ford's approach was to torque up to 20 – 25 Nm (15 – 18 lb. ft) while rotating the hub, then to back off half a turn and re-tighten using fingers and thumb. In the absence of a suitable dial gauge, this latter method should work here. The initial torque up will move the bearings against frictional resistance to a zero endfloat position, and the subsequent finger tightening will avoid any excessive preload. On this latter point, a toolmaker who worked at the Timex watch factory told me that on receipt of each new Schaublin lathe, one of their first actions was to wind up the spindle bearing preload to further increase the stiffness. Whether it caused

a reduction in life is not known.

The speed sensor was then located, and a quick check made to ensure that the disc would run correctly in the slot without fouling. (The slot is actually about 4mm wide, so will tolerate quite a bit of leeway.)

With this in place, the control panel housing can then be remounted, and its four screws fitted. The remaining components are then refitted, as a reversal of the dismantling procedure.

Initial experience

I did wonder whether it might be possible to gauge the improvement in rigidity due to the bearing change. In an earlier chapter, I described an inverted part off tool arrangement operated with the spindle running in reverse, and commented that when parting off with the tool, audible vibration could be detected. At the time I thought that a more substantial mounting bar for the tool might offer an improvement. However, after completing the bearing change, I used the same tool to part off steel bar, and this time there was no audible vibration effect. In fact it seemed to part off as sweetly as the rear toolpost on my Myford Super 7. Certainly there appears to be no downside regarding this modification; the machine runs as expected, just as smoothly to maximum speed. Perhaps a case of full marks to the original Russian designers.

Radius turning attachment

For applications in the amateur sector, these attachments usually feature a cutting tool, which may be set to a radius, and is then swept around the surface being generated. The sweeping action is typically controlled by a lever type handle, and

10.30. Radius turning attachment.

rotates about an axis, which for true spherical generation must intercept with the lathe spindle axis. Two main formats are in use, where the rotation axis may be either vertical (the handle moving horizontally), or horizontal as in this case. Traditionally, this is one of those devices which tended to be home constructed. Many designs have appeared from various authors over the years in not only MEW but also "Model Engineer", and suppliers such as Hemingway offer kits.

However, the competitive pricing of this item from Arc, does shift ones thinking along the make or buy spectrum, towards the buy decision. **Photo 10.30** shows the main components "out of the box and loosely assembled. The aluminium base plate brings the pivot line up close to lathe centre line height.

To fit the device to the lathe, the topslide is first removed, and the same fixing screws

used to hold down the aluminium base plate. The tool is then adjusted to give the desired radius, and locked in place. Here it could be found worth while measuring the swinging bracket **(Photo 10.31)** to obtain a datum dimension from outer face to pivot line, which might then be used for accurate adjustment of the tool tip position. In the photo, a piece of 8mm rod has been passed though the pivot holes and the measurement taken over this. 4mm is then deducted to give a reference dimension for zero radius.

Before fitting the base plate to the lathe, first check whether the centre screw for the cross side nut projects upward above the cross slide. Mine did, so it was screwed out a couple of turns, and a few thous filed off the top, before re-tightening.

If you intend to produce radii for aesthetic rather than accurate dimensional criteria, then forge ahead, fit the accessory with no more ado, and proceed to enjoy. However, if you wish to machine spherical parts to tight tolerances then there are a couple of easy modifications to upgrade the device. First check the pivot height. This is easily done as shown in **Photo 10.32**. A length of 8mm rod is mounted in the chuck, and one of the mounting brackets fitted and manoeuvred to bring its pivot bar close to the rod. The height of each can then be measured from the base plate. Ideally these should be identical, but most likely; production tolerances of the various components will stack up to create a slight mismatch. In my case, shimming up was required, and the quick and easy answer was to cut a couple of shims from thin

10.31. Measurement to establish reference.

10.32. Preparing to check pivot height.

card **(Photo 10.33).** Of course the best engineering solution would be metal shims, but for the relatively light forces involved, card, paper or Plasticard should all be viable. If the pivot height does not match the lathe centre height, then your radiused forms will not be truly spherical, but very slightly lemon shaped.

Another minor shortcoming, easily corrected, concerns the endfloat of the cast swinging frame on its pivots. For accurate work, it is useful to be able to position the cutting edge on centreline in plan. I added a wavy washer made as before from 0.8mm Mig welding wire, to the pivot farther from the operator, to bias the frame to the load side. In a similar manner, the tool location allows the bit some sideways movement. Limiting this movement and adding a micrometer feed for the toolbit will be upgrade exercises for another day.

Once the attachment is fitted and lined up at 90 degrees to the lathe axis, the cross slide is moved to bring the tool edge

10.33. A couple of thin card shims.

to centreline viewed in plan.

How you use the gadget will then depend on what you wish to produce. The radiused parts I have produced tend to be hemispherical ends e.g. for gas cylinder fittings. For this type of work, the tool radius may be set at the outset, then the saddle moved towards the chuck between "sweeps", under the control of the leadscrew handwheel, until the full form is achieved. Conversely, if the work is more nearly a sphere such as a ball handle, the pivot line position along the bed, must be set correctly from the start, and feeding

10.34. One of the shims in place.

10.35. Radiusing brass.

down to radius is accomplished either by moving the toolbit inwards between sweeps, or by commencing with the assembly positioned off centre towards the operator then progressively moving the cross slide inwards between sweeps, finishing on centre line. Note though, that this latter system may cause problems due to variation in effective tool cutting angles.

Photo 10.34 illustrates one of the shims in place with the unit fitted to the Mini-Lathe, and **Photo 10.35** shows work in progress to produce a radiused end produced on a piece of brass hex bar.

This brings to a conclusion this work on the Mini - Lathe, which I hope has opened up avenues for improving the performance, and extending the versatility of this increasingly popular little machine. Being a budget machine, it is likely for many purchasers to be a significant first or second step into the hobby of amateur or model engineering, and as such, the more convenience that can be incorporated and the more operations it can be persuaded to accommodate, the better. I hope that the book has demonstrated how with fairly straightforward and minor modifications, the Mini – Lathe can be transformed into an extremely versatile piece of kit, capable of serious and accurate small scale work.

INDEX

More Great Books from Fox Chapel Publishing

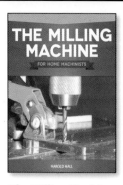

**The Milling Machine
for Home Machinists**
ISBN 978-1-56523-769-8 **$14.99**

**Metal Lathe for
Home Machinists**
ISBN 978-1-56523-693-6 **$12.95**

**Basic Lathework for
Home Machinists**
ISBN 978-1-56523-696-7 **$14.99**

**Milling for Home
Machinists**
ISBN 978-1-56523-694-3 **$12.95**

**The Metalworker's Workshop
for Home Machinists**
ISBN 978-1-56523-697-4 **$14.99**

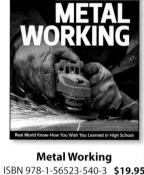

Metal Working
ISBN 978-1-56523-540-3 **$19.95**

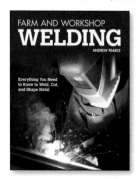

**Farm and
Workshop Welding**
ISBN 978-1-56523-741-4 **$24.99**

Drills and Drill Presses
ISBN 978-1-56523-472-7 **$9.95**

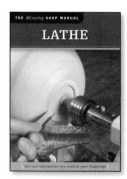

Lathe
ISBN 978-1-56523-773-5 **$12.95**

Look for These Books at Your Local Bookstore or Specialty Retailer
or at *www.FoxChapelPublishing.com*